ART CRIME AND SECURITY

By

James Lugarkemp

© 2022

SEINVARC PUBLISHING

Also by James Lugarkemp:

Security Theory & Key Practices

Black Swan Fraud

'...ten dollars from a vendor in the street. But I take it, I bury it in the sand for a thousand years, it becomes priceless.'

Rene Belloq

Preface

With all the human, health and environmental issues affecting our rapidly changing planet writing about the theft of art and antiquities would probably seem trivial to most. Many might see the art world as elitist, too many wealthy private collectors, too many museums displaying art that looks like art you have seen in another museum and too much art being bought and sold for extreme prices that the citizen on the street thinks is simply not justified. What can be tendered in mitigation to this viewpoint is that art is the history of our human evolution, the history of all our cultures and each piece of art and antiquity contributes to that. So because of that we must somehow find a way that it may never be lost.

It is difficult to articulate the importance of high-end art when most people do not have a stake in it or own a large collection of it. However, in a similar kind of way we all have a responsibility for things from the past more than we think – namely numerous family photographs, heirlooms and other possessions. Those things that families have on their mantlepiece or up in their loft, whether safely boxed up or unwittingly left amongst forgotten clutter. Those things that a family would never dream of throwing away because they are aware of their full historical family value and of course the most determining factor of all, that they are absolutely irreplaceable. Here is where you own personal family history can be remembered and shown to future generations without which they would have no visual appreciation, only your recollections.

Of course, most of these heirlooms, photographs, letters and so on would generally have no large monetary value to the outside world. But they still represent an evolution and ancestral timeline that is unique to a family that needs to be preserved, that needs to be shared with future generations. They are physical examples which are not really dissimilar to those intrinsic famous pieces of art and antiquity that are of historical value to a nation and its culture. But rather that these family heirlooms operate on a micro level because it is all valuable and it is all historical. Art is for all of us, owned by all of us and an incredibly important gateway to understanding the past, including our families.

I am not an art historian, academic, museum curator or casual collector and neither do I aspire to be. I am a security professional with an interest in art. You will know that when we visit a museum we do not place a value on art but rather what we get from it. How we see it and the feelings it musters within us is what gives a piece of art real value. You have probably had that feeling when you look at a painting of how you can quickly be inside the painting, standing on the landscape or next to the characters, some two or three hundred years ago. Sometimes I see the raised paint on a canvas, that 3D effect and realise I am looking at the paint that was actually brushed on by a world famous artist. Or the antiquities which may be prehistoric, Egyptian or Greek and Roman. Those antiquities made from using stone on stone that have a museum label underneath that says - around 12000BC. Or those Greek stone heads that always seem to be in plentiful supply, but where the noses always seem to be missing.

In writing this book I have concentrated on why, when we think of art and antiquities, there has been an historical problem of people feeling the need to steal it and deny some countries part of their cultural heritage. But also what is being done to protect art, or not. The first section of chapters will concentrate on five famous thefts from the 1900s to the 2000s, involving paintings with one related to antiquity. Looking in depth at the theft, why the art was taken, what was being done to protect it and how they were eventually recovered. One of the famous paintings taken, Woman in Gold, was part of Nazi looting during World War II and this is an entirely different and unforgivable aspect of art theft which seems to have been forgotten.

The second section deals with art and antiquities and all the problems that seem to follow. Chapters one and two will provide importance selected timelines for ancient civilisations, art history and techniques. Chapter three will look at antiquities, context and looting as well as antiquities in popular culture. Antiquities are the real life blood of national heritage and grave robbing or tomb raiding whatever you want to call it, still goes on today because quite simply they are buried in the ground. This looting in itself then distorts the timeline and true historical location for some antiquities. Unfortunately, with antiquities, social and political factors are always at play and this was not helped by Europeans in the early twentieth century and their popular pastime of travelling the world to acquire them legitimately or otherwise.

Chapter four moves onto paintings, seemingly the most popular art to steal. Popular maybe because of media and culture, maybe because there are so many of them to choose from or maybe because as you will see, they are so easy to take. It is crucial in the present day especially when we consider events from the past, to have an historical record of where art and especially an antiquity have come from. In chapter five provenance research is explained and how this is crucial when art moves between buyers and sellers and most importantly when acquired by museums. Having a detailed record of an actual item and how and when it is moved around and bought and sold, should be the only way art changes hands. Chapter six continues the theme of paintings with fakes, forgeries and science. Some fake paintings are just as famous as the originals because of their high quality as are the artists involved in an almost, production line scenario of output. The scientific methods developed over many years show how science is now helping academics, dealers, museums and governments to overcome wrong decision making when acquiring art and antiquities. Chapter seven will consider private art collections and money in art and how provenance is even more crucial here. The chapter includes details of the Royal Collection of which King Charles III is now custodian.

The third section offers an overarching view of the protection of art and how well it is being done. Chapter one and two highlight the always present curator vs security factor involved in the protection of art in museums and this has been ongoing for many years. The desire to have as many people as possible see the artwork, whilst simultaneously trying to stop someone stealing it. What law enforcement is doing worldwide and how the various agencies try to help both proactively and reactively. Then going back to museums, how emergency planning is protecting art from environmental factors such as fire and flooding. The last chapter is on art and insurance and why this is an important, but little talked about subject matter, in the art world.

How do they get the stolen art and antiquities back and how successful they are is discussed in section four with chapters on art law and art repatriation and recovery. There have been numerous issues over the years with private collectors, museums and countries regarding repatriation and recovery. With some of those issues quite complicated in that governments will argue art and particularly antiquities should never have left their country in the first place. With some museums arguing the antiquities were acquired legitimately, have a good provenance and may have been lost forever if not for their guardianship, which for some antiquities could have been for over a hundred years. For other art stolen much has never been recovered, but with the challenging work undertaken by law enforcement and other agencies there have been successes.

Many of these issues emanate from a piece of history seemingly not known to everyone and arguably forgotten about by so many, the mass art theft programme of all time. Nazi looting and collecting of art and antiquities during World War II was an unstoppable machine, with lives destroyed, personal artworks stolen and those numerous family heirlooms lost forever. The mass of Nazi machinery behind it all is beguiling so this chapter will look at the framework of the Third Reich, the hierarchy leading the art theft, why they were so interested in it all and how they went about it. The chapter is written in the style of a file from the Office of Strategic Services in 1945, the wartime forerunner of the CIA with reference to the Monuments Men. Whether the good people, be that in law enforcement, committed governments or museum directors, with a clear moral compass in what they already own or acquire in the future, can indeed stay ahead of the crime curve, remains to be seen.

In all the pages that follow, the aim of this book has always been to bring together the main generic elements of the subject matters of art crime, security and art recovery, which the reader can find elsewhere, with a longer narrative and in greater academic detail, if they so wish.

James Lugarkemp

Cambridge

2022

x

Contents

FIVE FAMOUS THEFTS 1

Chapter 1 France 2

Chapter 2 United States 12

Chapter 3 Norway 27

Chapter 4 Peru 39

Chapter 5 Austria 45

ART CRIME 55

Chapter 1 Select Ancient Civilisations and Biblical Timeline 56

Chapter 2 Select Art Movements, Techniques, Architecture and Art 63

Chapter 3 Antiquities 74

Chapter 4 Theft of Art 92

Chapter 5 Provenance Research 97

Chapter 6 Fakes, Forgeries and Science 103

Chapter 7 Private Collectors, the Royal Collection and Art Money 111

SECURITY 118

Chapter 1 Museum Security 119

Chapter 2 Law Enforcement 127

Chapter 3 Emergency Planning and Response for Art 134

Chapter 4 Art and Insurance 140

REPATRIATION AND RECOVERY **145**
Chapter 1 Office of Strategic Services File – 1945 146
Chapter 2 Art and Law 163
Chapter 3 Repatriation and Recovery 167

FIVE FAMOUS THEFTS

Chapter 1
France

Museum - Louvre

The Louvre is an art museum and historical monument in Paris, France. Originally the Louvre Castle and located mainly on the right side of the River Seine, it was a medieval castle built during two decades from 1190 under the orders of King Phillip II of France. Phillip ruled between 1180 and 1223 and helped transform France into the most prosperous and powerful nation in Europe. He checked the power of nobles and assisted towns in freeing themselves from feudal lords. Granted privileges and liberties to the emerging cultured middle and upper classes, as well as reorganising the French government. All of which helped bring financial and social stability. Before his departure for the Third Crusade, to help recapture Jerusalem along with other western European powers in 1190, he wanted to further reinforce the walls he had already built around Paris. This would offer Paris additional protection from invasion. The castle wall enclosure which bears his name, completed a squared fortress with ten defensive towers surrounded by a moat. The castle had two entrances with the main one facing the Seine, protected by drawbridges and framed between two twin towers. Two additional buildings housing the garrison and armoury were located outside this enclosure.

The castle eventually lost its defensive function due to, amongst other things, urban expansion and in 1546 it was converted into a palace as the primary residence of the French kings. The building was subsequently extended many times. In 1682 King Louis XIV broke with convention and chose the Palace of Versailles twenty kilometres southwest of Paris as the new royal residence. Leaving the Louvre primarily as a place to display the royal art collection. In 1692 and for the next one hundred years, up until the first French Republic, the Louvre was home to two learned societies from the Academy of the Institute of France. In the early 1790s the new revolutionary National Assembly decreed the Louvre should be used as museum to display national treasures. The museum opened in 1793 with an exhibition of 537 paintings, with the majority of the works being part of the royal collection or confiscated church property. The collection was increased under Napoleon and the museum renamed Museum Napoleon. However, after his abdication many works seized by his armies were rightly returned to their original owners, providing an early example of regime art theft. The collection was then further increased during subsequent royal reigns and during the second French Republic. By the early 1900s the Louvre housed one of the finest art collections in the world. At the head of its operations were an elite core of intellectuals and establishment figures appointed by the government.

Artist - Leonardo da Vinci

He was born as Leonardo di ser Piero Vinci in April 1452 in Florence Italy. He was a polymath of the High Renaissance era known for his painting, drawing, sculpting, science, engineering, architecture and anatomy. He was educated at the studio of the renowned Italian painter Andrea del Verrocchio and spent the last three years of his life in France, where he died in 1519. His studies in science and engineering are considered impressive and innovative. These studies were recorded in notebooks of 13000 pages. They were written throughout his life and travels as he made continual observations of the world around him. Despite recent awareness and admiration of him as a scientist and inventor, his initial fame rested on his achievements as an artist and painter, with fewer than twenty known works completed. Four classic works in popular culture by Leonardo (amongst numerous others in both painting and science) are The Vitruvian Man, The Last Supper, Salvator Mundi and the Mona Lisa.

The Vitruvian Man c1490 is a drawing which represents the Leonardo concept of the ideal human body proportions. His drawing of a human inside the parameters of a circle and a square, are taken from a description by Roman architect Vitruvius. However, Leonardo decided to represent his own proportions rather than those provided by Vitruvius. By measuring a number of male models in Milan the drawing represents his believe that the human body is an analogy for the workings of the universe. The Last Supper c1492-1498 was made famous most recently with its depiction in the film The Da Vinci Code, 2003. The painting represents the scene of the Last Supper of Jesus, along with his twelve disciples and depicts the consternation that occurred amongst the disciples when Jesus announced that one of them would later betray him.

Salvator Mundi c1500 is one of the most copied Leonardo paintings with about twelve known examples executed by his pupils and others. The painting shows Jesus making a sign of the cross with his right hand whilst holding a transparent crystal ball in his left. This is signalling his role as Salvator Mundi Latin for, saviour of the world and representing the celestial sphere of the heavens. It was sold at auction for $450.3 million in November 2017 by Christies Auctioneers in New York. It set a new record for the most expensive painting ever sold at a public auction. It has since been posited that bidding was done on behalf of Saudi Arabian crown prince Mohammed bin Salman. The current location of the painting is reported as unknown. As of 2019 reports stated that it may have been in storage in Switzerland although it has been rumoured to be stored on his luxury private superyacht Serene, one of the largest in the world. The Mona Lisa c1503 has been described as the best known, most visited and most written about work of art in the world. This is due to its ground-breaking qualities such as the enigmatic expression, composition, layering and subtle modelling of body form. It was stolen in 1911.

Painting - Mona Lisa

It has been suggested by academics that the painting is of Lisa del Giocondo an Italian noble women, with the portrait being commissioned by her husband. An oil painting on wooden panel, it was acquired by King Francis I of France and is now the property of the French Republic and has been on permanent display in the Louvre since 1797. It is probably the most valuable painting in the world and holds the Guinness world record for the highest known insurance valuation in history at US$100 million in 1962, equivalent to $660 million as of 2019.

The ability of Leonardo to create the mystic of the Mona Lisa, was by way of developing new techniques in painting and in particular a technique he described as sfumato. It gave the painting a smoked or veiled effect and means you encounter the subject almost through a mist and thus it is difficult to interpret what the model is thinking. Expression is determined largely by the position of the corners of the human eyes and mouth. With this painting Leonardo has blurred the corners of both eyes and mouth, thus making it difficult to be sure exactly what the expression is. As a result of that indecision the viewer comes to their own interpretation of the expression. A further technique making the painting unique is that whilst the face is looking at you in a straight line, the body is seated slightly at an angle, so the model is almost in a conventional pose, whilst at the same time moving and turning her body.

Person of Interest

Vincenzo Peruggia was born in 1881 near Como, northern Italy. He moved to France just prior to the theft in 1911 and like many Italians was simply in search of work. He lived in a small apartment in northeast central Paris near the Gare de l'Est railway station. He had had a challenging time settling in and his French neighbours were not welcoming of Italian nationals and less so of their cultural differences. He spoke French in a faltering way and experienced all the problems of immigration in that period and this had affected him. At first he struggled to find work but his skills as a carpenter eventually paid off. He secured a very significant job in the Louvre as part of a team of four people responsible for installing the glass coverings on paintings. So, he had actually handled the Mona Lisa with his team at some point to carry out this very task. In later life and after the theft Peruggia was released from prison, fought in the war, married and moved back to France to work as a decorator. He died in October 1925.

Theft

The Louvre was no stranger to threats against its artwork. Anonymous letters targeting specific pictures had been received in previous years but these had been dismissed by senior museum figures as not credible. There had also been some minor thefts from the building but nothing of note, however, these patterns were ignored and for all intents and purposes security at the museum was not tightened or future incidents planned for. This may have been because the Louvre had reason to feel secure because they employed almost an army of security staff to inhabit the entrances and galleries. However, behind the uniforms there was deep discontent. The security staff of the museum were not professional museum operatives, they were veteran soldiers sent there by the French war department, as a retirement posting. Some were bitter service personnel, some were alcoholics, most of them slept on duty at the museum, some went out of the museum without the knowledge of the management. They were great in number but painfully low in operational quality and personal responsibility.

The Louvre was open to the public for six days of the week. Monday was assigned for closure to facilitate behind the scenes activities such as cleaning and maintenance. Departmental staff would also tend to the art and antiquities whether repair, photography or movement between galleries or the basement reserve. This is the kind of activity that goes on in museums to this day. Whereby they remain, largely, open to the public at weekends but for logistical and security reasons assign a day for this work. There would have been a number of staff around at the Louvre on the Monday busily working, but under no security supervision, on valuable art and antiquities.

On Monday 21st August 1911 the day of the theft, there were only ten security staff covering the whole museum and the previous week had been busy at the Louvre. None of these ten security staff were positioned in the Salon Carre, the great gallery and the largest in the Louve where the most valuable and prestigious Italian paintings were kept. At around 06:00 am that morning Vincenzo Peruggia left his apartment. He had planned the theft of the Mona Lisa, although it has been suggested he spent Sunday night at the museum hidden away in a small store. Although he no longer now worked for the museum people still knew him, so why his presence on the day of the theft was not questioned by any member of staff or security, is unknown. When Peruggia arrives he simply walked straight into the museum as the main gate is open and unattended. Once inside it becomes obvious to him that the galleries were deserted, on a day of closure when the public would assume people behind the scenes would be busy at work. He then entered the gallery and proceeded to remove the Mona Lisa from the wall armed with the knowledge of how it was attached to the wall, how to remove it, how heavy it was and how to carry it. Peruggia then leaves the gallery with the painting but is still fortunate that nobody notices him. He is dressed like a member of staff and so blends in nicely. He takes full advantage of the lacklustre approach to security by the museum which should never have been taken for granted, even when it is closed to the public.

Peruggia then carries the painting to a small staircase nearby and removes the painting from the frame and glass covering which he had only a year before placed over the painting as part of his employment. He then leaves both in this staircase area. He now has the painting on the wooden panel on which it was painted and covers it with a cloth and moves to the bottom of the staircase to exit the museum via a small door, which he initially believed would be open, but he now finds locked. Peruggia maintaining his calm then begins to try and remove the whole door lock by unscrewing its surround with the same screwdriver with which he had removed the Mona Lisa. A museum plumber who knows Peruggia then walks past but the thief maintains his cool. He then converses with the plumber that someone has locked the door and the plumber then advises him that he has a key and lets him out. There was one more barrier in his way, a museum side gate known as the Porte de Louvre. This would normally be guarded by security but the gate was again unstaffed and left ajar. Whereupon Peruggia walks out onto the Paris streets and the theft of the most famous painting in the world, then and now, is complete.

Peruggia weaved through the streets of Paris with the painting under his arm, wrapped in the cloth and immediately goes back to his apartment, a small run down building near the railway station. He arrives there at about 08:00 hrs relieved that his mission has been successful and no doubt amused his small apartment now contains a masterpiece. Twenty four hours after he had left the museum still no one is aware the painting has been stolen. At 10:00 hrs the following day the museum opens to the public as normal. One of the first visitors is an artist named Louis Beroud. He has travelled to the museum to paint his own interpretation of the Mona Lisa and heads straight to the gallery, looks up and finds nothing but an empty space on the wall. He then goes and enquires with a museum security officer, who then seeks advice from other staff members, but even then there is still a lack of real concern. A short time after security personnel return showing signs of panic that a painting that has been in the museum for over one hundred years has now gone. The museum leadership, police and the Paris authorities are then alerted. The museum and its vicinity is then put into an immediate lockdown.

French police then waste neither time or extensive resources, of around two hundred officers, in searching the Louvre and its environs and then interviewing staff and security. However, the police were alerted and did not become fully involved until it was too late and before long the trail has gone cold. Whether staff who may or may not have seen anything were purposely keeping quiet for fear of their own livelihoods cannot be known. But interviews were not in any way fruitful for the French police, providing no leads whatsoever. Eventually police discover the discarded frame and glass on the stairway. Not long into the late afternoon the theft is headline news in Paris and the Louvre is closed until further notice. Headlines described the theft as a national disaster.

In leaving the glass and the frame Peruggia also leaves a fingerprint. Police knew he had worked at the Louvre and already had a criminal record. At this time French police relied more on descriptive identification of suspects such as body measurements, scars and tattoos with substantially less emphasis on fingerprints. Hence, they only kept one set of fingerprints on each police custody record and this was for the right hand. The print left by Peruggia was that of the thumb on his left hand. The other error made by police is that they did not interview the men who worked, or had worked, for the company who fitted the glass over the paintings, including Peruggia. For two years little is heard about the whereabouts of the Mona Lisa or indeed how the police investigation was proceeding, if at all. During this period Peruggia is still in Paris and keeping a low profile, little is known about his activities or employment during that time.

Then in November 1913 a letter postmarked from Paris arrives in Florence, Italy. It was addressed to an eminent city art dealer Alfredo Geri and signed Leonardo. The letter from Peruggia offered up the Mona Lisa and he is intrigued. Geri mentions the letter to the then director of the Uffizi Gallery who tells him to answer the letter, as it was presenting the return of the Mona Lisa for the Italian nation, with no mention of money. So by return letter Peruggia (Leonardo!) is invited to Florence. Peruggia on receipt of the letter packs the Mona Lisa into a trunk and travels to Florence and for the first time in over three centuries the Mona Lisa leaves France. Peruggia eventually arrives in Florence and books into a small hotel and pushes the trunk under his bed for the night. The next morning he is to meet Geri and the director of the Uffizi. The two men then attended the hotel room of Peruggia and he retrieves the trunk and produces the Mona Lisa. They then compare the painting with photographs of the Mona Lisa which show all its intricacies and after a short time have no doubt it is the original. They then persuade Peruggia to let them take the painting away to place in the Ufizzi and on leaving the hotel they call the Carabinieri, who then attend the hotel and arrest Peruggia, who is subsequently charged and sent to trial.

Peruggia was convicted at his trial and sentenced to just over one year in a Florence prison. He informed the court in line with his letter, that his motives were entirely nationalistic and (despite numerous letters to other parties) suggests he always wanted the Mona Lisa to hang in the Ufizzi Gallery. However, most Italian people did not consider him a hero. They actually considered him no more than a stupid small time thief, who could have caused irreparable damage to the Mona Lisa, during those two years that it was missing from the Louvre.

Chapter 2
United States

Museum – Isabella Stewart Gardner

The Isabella Stewart Gardner Museum (ISGM) in Boston, New England houses a significant collection of around 2500 paintings, sculptures, tapestries, and decorative arts. It was founded by Isabella Stewart Gardner and her will decreed that her art collection be forever continually exhibited. The building of the museum was completed in 1901. Isabella Stewart was born in New York City in 1840 and she was the daughter of a wealthy linen merchant and became a leading American art collector and philanthropist. She attended Grace Church School in Manhattan where she studied art, music, French and Italian, which collectively ignited her interest in art. At sixteen she and her family moved to Paris where she was enrolled in a school for American girls and her classmates included members of the wealthy Gardner family of Boston. After returning to the United States her former classmate Julia Gardner invited her to Boston where she was introduced to her brother, Jack Gardner, one of the most eligible bachelors in the city. They later married and then lived in a house that her father gave them, in Boston. In the late 1880s they travelled frequently across America, Europe and Asia keeping, them out of the country for an overall total of ten years. They discovered foreign cultures and expanded their knowledge of art as well as their collection. The earliest works in the Gardner collection were accumulated, in particular, during their trips to Europe as she concentrated on European paintings after inheriting $1.75 million from her father, which is well in excess of $60 million today.

Isabella and her husband recognized that their house in Boston although already enlarged, was not sufficient to house their growing collection of art. After the sudden death of her husband in 1898, Isabella sought to realise their shared dream of, a building, to house their treasured art collection and so purchased land. She hired an architect to build a museum, modelled on the renaissance palaces of Venice, with a glass covered garden courtyard. Gardner then spent a year carefully installing her collection according to her personal preferences with gallery installations, antiquities, paintings, sculptures, textiles and furniture from different periods and cultures. The museum had a grand opening celebration in January 1903, featuring the Boston Symphony Orchestra. It opened to the general public a few months later. Isabella continued to expand the collection and arrange it until she died in 1924, whereupon she left the museum a $3.6 million endowment.

By the 1980s the museum was running low on funds and its overall financial situation had left the building in a poor condition. It lacked a climate control system, insurance cover and needed basic building maintenance. After the Federal Bureau of Investigation (FBI) uncovered a plot by Boston criminals to steal art from the museum in 1982, the museum allocated what available funds it had to improve security. Among the improvements were to be sixty infrared motion detectors and a CCTV system consisting of four cameras placed around the building perimeter. However, there were to be no cameras installed within the building, as museum trustees thought installing the equipment in such a historical building would be too expensive. Another recommendation was that more security staff should be employed. Despite the proposed security improvements the only way police could be summoned to the museum was with a panic button, under the main security desk. For example, at the time other museums had fail-safe systems which required night security to make hourly phone calls to the police to indicate all was well, but not the ISGM. Subsequently, an independent security consultant had reviewed the museums operations in 1988 and determined they were on a par with most other museums, but still recommended improvements. Because of the potential financial strain on the museum coupled with the wishes of Isabella against renovations and altering the aesthetics of the museum, the trustees did not approve the security enhancements. Crucially, the trustees also denied a request from the security manager for higher security staff salaries, in a bid to attract better qualified and more professional operatives.

Artists and the Art

A total of thirteen pieces of art including one antiquity were stolen. The FBI initially estimated the value of the haul at $200 million but had raised this estimate to $500-600 million by the turn of the century, the second highest value art theft ever. The theft involved an unusual mix of stolen items and while some paintings were valuable, the thieves passed on other valuable works, as well as deciding to take art of substantially less relative value. As the will of Isabella decreed nothing in her collection should be moved. The empty frames for the stolen paintings remain hanging in their respective locations in the hope of any eventual return. Despite the quality of the museum collection its funding was low and there was no insurance cover in place. This was, in the main, due to the fact they were irreplaceable works and therefore museum leaders believed any insurance pointless. The selection of works and the overly robust way in which the thieves handled the art, led the FBI and other law enforcement agencies to believe these thieves were not experts commissioned to steal particular works, but rather common criminals acting on instructions.

Jan Vermeer - The Concert

This painting accounted for approximately half of the value of the entire theft and was valued at around $250 million at that time. Vermeer who will be discussed at greater length in a later chapter was a Dutch painter born in 1632. Due to the availability of only thirty four known works in the world, every Vermeer comes with a high price tag. The Concert has been dated to the 1660s and shows three musicians - a young woman sitting at a harpsicord, a man playing the lute and a woman who is singing. The upturned lid of the harpsicord is decorated with an idyllic simple landscape, with its bright colouring standing in contrast to the two paintings hanging on the wall to their left and right. Whilst their clothing and surroundings seem to identify them as members of the bourgeoisie. A viol stringed instrument can also be seen lying in the foreground on a luxurious black and white marbled floor. It was acquired by Isabella at a Paris auction for $5,000 in 1892.

Rembrandt –

The Storm on the Sea of Galilee, A Lady and Gentleman in Black, a Self-Portrait

Rembrandt was a Dutch painter, printmaker and draughtsman born in 1606. His work depicted a wide range of styles and subject matter including portraits, self-portraits, landscapes, historical, biblical and mythological themes. After a successful apprenticeship Rembrandt started his own workshop and he then opened a studio in Leiden, north-west Netherlands around 1624. He later moved to Amsterdam, a city rapidly expanding as the new business capital of the Netherlands. Here he began to practice as a professional portraitist for the first time, with great success. The storm on the Sea of Galilee is an oil on canvas painting dated around 1633. The painting depicts the biblical story of Jesus calming the storm on the sea, as is described in the bible. The painting is in vertical format and shows the disciples of Christ struggling desperately against the heavy storm to regain control of their fishing boat, as a huge wave strikes the bow and rips apart one of the sails. A disciple is seen vomiting over the side. Another looking directly out from the scene, on the boat itself, is Rembrandt himself. Christ can be seen on the right of the artist and is the only one who remains calm. It has since been estimated to be worth around $140 million. A Lady and Gentleman in Black is another 1633 painting, also oil on canvas and depicts a well-dressed husband and wife. The stolen self-portrait is a small postage stamp-sized self-portrait etching and had been previously stolen and then returned in 1970.

Govert Flinck - Landscape with Obelisk

Flinck was a painter born in 1615, just across the now Netherlands border with Germany, who also had a strong interest in drawing and etching. Eventually living in Amsterdam for many years, Flinck followed the style of Rembrandt in all the works which he executed between 1636 and 1648 and was acknowledged as one of his best pupils. This explains why the painting was formerly attributed to Rembrandt until the 1980s and it has been suggested as one of the reasons why perhaps, it was mistakenly stolen from the ISGM. The painting is dated as 1638 and is oil on wood. The painting is a stormy scene with a dramatically lit obelisk (very high tapering stone pillar) in the middle ground. Just outside Amsterdam there were indeed two obelisks that marked territorial boundaries, however, this scene with distant mountains and dense trees looks nothing like the Netherlands.

Edouard Manet – Chez Tortoni

Manet was a French painter born into an upper class family in 1832 who became engrossed in the world of painting from an early age. From 1850 to 1856 Manet studied under the academic painter Thomas Couture and in his spare time copied paintings in the Louvre. During this period Manet visited Germany, Italy and the Netherlands and was influenced by a number of painters. Manet then opened his own studio in Paris. Chez Tortoni was painted around 1875 and is oil on canvas. The painting depicts an unidentified gentleman sitting at a table in the Cafe Tortoni de Paris, whilst drawing on a sketchpad with a half-empty glass of beer sitting on the table.

Edgar Degas –

La Sortie de Pesage, Cortege aux Environs de Florence, Program for an Artistic Soirée 1, Program for an Artistic Soirée 2 and Three Mounted Jockeys

Degas was a French painter born in 1834 and famous for his pastel drawings and oil paintings and production of sculptures, prints and drawings. Degas began painting early in life and after graduating from school, had already turned a room in his home into a painters studio. He then registered as a copyist in the Louvre Museum. Degas has been described as a classical painter of modern life and especially identified with the subject of dance, with more than half of his work depicting dancers. Degas painted racehorses and jockeys and his other portraits are notable for their complexity and particularly their portrayal of human isolation. Five sketches were stolen from the ISGM and they were each done on paper less than a square foot in size and made with pencils, inks, and charcoals. They are of relatively little value compared with the other stolen works and worth less than $100,000 combined, however, all still unique and irreplaceable.

Gu and French Imperial Eagle

A Gu is a type of ancient Chinese bronze vessel used to drink or offer wine during ceremonial rituals. About 10 inches tall the beaker was one of the oldest works in the museum dating to the Shang Dynasty in the 12th century BC. The estimated value of the antiquity was several thousand dollars. The French Imperial Eagle was a golden finial from the corner of a framed flag from the Imperial Guard of Napoleon. A $100,000 reward was offered at the time for information leading to the return of this finial alone.

Persons of Interest

Investigators have called the case unique for its lack of strong physical evidence such as fingerprints, footprints and DNA. The two persons committing (what was technically a robbery) the theft were disguised as police officers. The museum security guards and witnesses in the street described one thief as white male, about 5F10 in his early 30s with a medium build, dark eyes, dark hair and wearing gold wire rim glasses. The other as white male, 6F01, in his mid-30s, dark eyes and dark hair with both men wearing fake moustaches. There was no further leads or evidence on the actual identity of the two thieves. In subsequent court documents in 2013, the two suspected of being the thieves were named as George Reissfelder and Lenny DiMuzio both of whom died later in 1991, Reissfelder from a drug overdose whilst DiMuzio was murdered. Both were suspected of having organised crime connections and the brother of Reissfelder later recalled seeing a painting similar to the Chez Tortoni hanging on the wall of his apartment, although this remains unproven.

Rick Abath

Museum security operative Rick Abath was investigated early on by the FBI. This was because of his suspicious behaviour on the night of the theft which included, shutting down a fire panel, momentarily opening the side door of the museum twenty minutes prior to the theft and moving away from his panic button situated under his security desk, when the thieves entered the museum. He was also the only person located on the motion detector system in the Blue Room Gallery from which the Manet was taken, despite the thieves having also been in that gallery. Its frame was subsequently found discarded at the main security desk. Abath had always protested his innocence and denied any involvement and there has never been enough evidence for the FBI to bring a prosecution. However, some commentators consider him to have been the insider for the theft.

Myles Connor

Connor is a native of Massachusetts and prior to the theft had been a convicted criminal since the 1960s, for offences including drugs and art theft. At the time of the ISGM theft he was in prison. Connor admitted to having previously committed about thirty art thefts and that stealing from the ISGM had indeed been on his wish list. Connor is considered by some to have been the biggest art thief in the United States and known as someone who likes, knows and collects art. Connor has always denied any involvement and there has never been enough evidence for the FBI to bring a prosecution. However, some commentators consider him to have been the main planner, organiser and facilitator of the theft, regardless that he was in prison.

Bill Youngworth

Youngworth is former art dealer and connoisseur and an expert in antiques, fine art and diamonds. He has a long criminal record and was a long-time friend of Myles Connor. At the time of the ISGM theft Youngworth had criminal connections in Boston, was close to bankruptcy, had a drug problem and was storing the art collection of Connor. But like him was in prison when the theft took place but was released shortly afterwards. He was then involved in a very public negotiator role for the potential return of the stolen art in 1997. However, some commentators consider him to have also been the sender of a letter to the museum in 1994, concerning again negotiation for return of the art which was a much more secretive undertaking. He is also considered as being the second planner, organiser and facilitator of the theft alongside Connor, regardless that he was also in (a different) prison at the time.

Bobby Donati

Career criminal Donati was murdered in 1991 in the midst of a gang war within the Patriarca organised crime family of which he was a member. According to Myles Connor Donati had worked with him on past art thefts and claimed the two had previously conducted reconnaissance on the ISGM. Where Donati had took a particular interest in the Napoleonic finial. Many commentators consider him to have been heavily involved in the organisation of the ISGM theft. But as to how much the bosses of the Patriarca family were actually aware of his activities and indeed involved themselves, is still unknown.

Whitey Bulger

Bulger was one of the most powerful crime bosses in Boston during the era. He headed the Winter Hill Gang which was a rival to the

Patriarca crime family. In the early months his name was heavily linked to the ISGM theft. He claimed he did not organize the theft and had in fact sent out some of his associates in an attempt to determine who had carried out the theft, on his territory, without his authorisation, so he could be paid a fee. Despite the high profile name of Bulger and his activities there has never been any FBI evidence of his involvement or that of the Winter Hill Gang. Many commentators have suggested his involvement in the theft and his connections with the Irish Republican Army (IRA) and their alleged involvement. With suggestions Bulger had taken some of the paintings to the IRA in Ireland and this is a theory that has seen longevity. However, Richard O'Rawe a former high ranking member of the IRA stated they had nothing to do with the theft and that the IRA were at the time raking in a great deal of money domestically. So we can assume the possibility of acquiring paintings for use as ransom or collateral in their activities, would not have been in their plans at that time.

Theft

The thirteen works of art were stolen in the early morning hours of Sunday 18th March 1990. The two security staff on duty for the night shift were music students supplementing their studies. Rick Abath was the experienced security staff, the other undertaking his very first night shift. The security procedure maintained that one security patrolled the galleries, with a radio and torch, while the other sat at the security desk. Abath was the first to patrol during which fire alarms sounded off in different locations in the museum, but he could not locate any fire or smoke. Abath then returned to the security room where he said the fire alarm panel indicated smoke in multiple locations. He assumed some type of malfunction and surprisingly, shut the panel down. He then went back on patrol and before he completed his rounds made a stop at the side entrance of the museum, briefly opening the side door and shutting it again, allegedly making sure it was operating correctly. However this was not normal procedure. The security manager would not have permitted his staff to do this and he did not tell his colleague he was doing this or why. It was later suggested this was a signal to the thieves. Abath then completed the rest of his patrol and returned to the security desk around 01:00 am, at which point his colleague began his patrol.

At about 01:20 am two persons approached the side entrance of the museum. Abath was sitting at a security desk near to the main entrance monitoring the outside CCTV, whilst the other security conducted a patrol. The two thieves dressed as police officer's then pressed the side entrance intercom and then showed fake police badges toward the side entrance camera. The thieves claimed they were responding to a disturbance in the rear grounds of the museum. However, there was no procedure or protocol as to how security were to respond to police arriving at this particular entrance and wanting to gain entry to the museum. Abath then pressed the door release and the thieves entered, he then buzzes them through two further security doors.

Once at the security desk they ask that the other security operative be called back to the desk. They then somehow get Abath to move away from the desk, underneath which is situated a panic button direct to the Boston Police Department. With the two security now together they are overpowered and taken down to the basement area and tied, some distance apart, to pipework. They are bound with duct tape over their faces both across and down, meaning they can neither see nor speak. The internal museum alarms were not set up to activate with an increase in unusual activity, they would only tigger in relation to external activity within its immediate boundaries. So the thieves were now free to roam the museum. They moved around all floors of the museum, seemingly undecided on what needed to be stolen.

In the Dutch gallery on the first floor, where the Vermeer and Rembrandt were located, as the thieves approached the paintings a device began beeping. This would normally trip when a visitor was too close to a painting. It was immediately smashed by the thieves. They took the two main Rembrandt paintings and threw them on the marble floor which shattered their glass frames, they then cut the canvases out of their frames. The thieves took the small postage size self-portrait etching. On the right side of the room they removed the Flinck and Vermeer from their frames. The final piece taken from the room was an ancient Chinese gu antiquity. The thieves then entered a narrow hallway, known as the Short Gallery, on the other end of the first floor and took the exposed eagle finial atop the flagpole. They also took the five Degas sketches from this gallery. The last work stolen was the Manet from the Blue Room on the ground floor. However, the museum motion detectors did not detect any movement within the Blue Room during their time in the building. Only movement from Rick Abath during the two occasions he passed through the gallery on his earlier patrol.

As they prepared to leave the thieves checked on the two security, then moved to the office of the security manager. Here they took the video cassettes that recorded their entrance on the CCTV and the data printouts from the motion detection equipment. Fortunately for law enforcement the motion detection data was still captured on a hard drive, which remained untouched. The thieves then took the stolen items out of the museum via the same side entrance doors. The theft lasted eighty-one minutes and after two trips to their vehicle they drove off through the streets of Boston, with a haul worth half a billion dollars.

The early security shift arrived later in the morning, realizing something was wrong when they could not establish contact with anyone inside the museum to gain access. They called in the security director of the museum, who upon entering the building with his keys, found nobody at the main security desk. Police were immediately called, who on arrival searched the building until they found the night security still tied up in the basement.

A number of law enforcement agencies collaborated at the museum, which was carefully examined, with the FBI involved as they were, sure that the stolen art would cross federal lines. Both security staff were interviewed at length. Rick Abath had insisted to investigators that he was on point the night of the theft with his duties but had just made a very unfortunate misjudgement. Others in law enforcement take the view that it was a collective failure in that security staff were poorly trained, there were ineffective security protocols and procedures, security systems were low grade, the museum had no money and for the reason already stated, no insurance. The FBI proceeded full on with the investigation and despite generic descriptions of the thieves and no forensic evidence they initially felt the investigation was progressing, as they followed up leads and interviews and eliminated some individuals. Within three days the director of the ISGM solicited help from Sotheby's and Christie's auction houses to post a of $1 million reward for information leading to the return of the paintings, without success. The theft subsequently went down in Boston folklore, with specific local organised crime gangs and other criminals allegedly connected with it, in one way or another.

Four years later in 1994, the museum director received an anonymous printed letter from someone attempting to negotiate with them for the return of the stolen art. The writer explained that they were a third party who had contact with the thieves and that the paintings had not been sold on but were being kept safe in the correct archival conditions. However, he wanted $2 million for his work. The negotiator also wanted immunity for themselves, the thieves and any other party involved in the theft. The person stated that if the ISGM were keen to accept the offer, they should print a coded message in the Boston Globe newspaper. Believing this to be a good lead the ISGM immediately passed the letter to the FBI. The coded message, which was to be the number 1 printed in a particular column, was sent in the Sunday 1st May 1994 edition. A week later the ISGM received a second letter in which the negotiator acknowledged the museum was interested in the deal. But they had become fearful of increased undercover activity and investigation by the FBI and other law enforcement agencies in the days since contact had been made. The ISGM never heard from the writer again.

Two years later around March 1996, the federal statute of limitation expired so the thieves and anyone else who had participated in the theft could no longer be prosecuted. As the years passed the FBI kept a number of agents on the case in the hope of a breakthrough. But despite hundreds of interviews and the chasing down of countless leads, none came. It was believed at this point that the paintings were still located somewhere in New England.

The reward for information resulting in the return of the paintings was increased to $5 million in the summer of 1997. At this point Bill Youngworth came forward to confirm he could provide that and facilitate their return. However, he wanted a blanket amnesty from prosecution for any offences connected to the theft as part of the arrangement, this was refused by the FBI. On Wednesday 27th August 1997 the Boston Herald ran a headline story saying one of their reporters had seen the Storm on the Sea of Galilee painting. That reporter Tom Mashberg had been taken blindfolded by persons unknown to a remote warehouse. He was taken upstairs to a storage locker where a rolled up canvas was pulled out, which looked like the Rembrandt. The next step was that Youngworth supposedly met with officials from the ISGM in New York City, from which he was paid a small advance on the reward. This was subsequently denied by the ISGM, but that the actual meeting itself took place, they did not.

Shortly after, an envelope arrived from New York at the offices of the Boston Herald, containing paint chippings. Testing then took place and for obvious reasons the assumption was that the chippings were from the Rembrandt. But this was dismissed when examiners found the paint was missing a particular varnish that Rembrandt used on his painting during the period the Storm was painted. What they did acknowledge was that the chippings in their pigmentation, colour and characteristics were completely consistent, but with the stolen Vermeer not the Rembrandt. However, the FBI wanted the return of the Vermeer as an initial good will measure before proceeding with any further negotiations. The return of the painting did not materialise. So at this point no further action was taken by the ISGM or law enforcement.

Within three months Youngworth was back in prison, on an unrelated matter, thus his role as a possible intermediary at an abrupt end. In 2017, some twenty seven years after the theft, the reward was doubled to $10 million with an expiration date set for the end of the year. This reward was extended following increased information being received by the FBI from the public. It is the largest reward ever offered by a private institution and was for information that leads directly to the recovery of all the stolen art and in good condition. At the time of writing the stolen art has still not been recovered and the investigation by the FBI has proved to be one of their most expensive and longest running ever. They are no longer concerned with the capture and prosecution of those involved (remembering too the expired statute limitations) but rather the safe return of all the stolen art.

Chapter 3
Norway

Museum – Munch

The Munch Museum as of 2021 is in a new building located in Bjorvika, on a waterfront area next to the Oslo Opera House, south-east of Oslo, Norway. It is dedicated to the life and works of the Norwegian artist Edvard Munch. Previously, it was to be found at Toyen in the old town of Oslo city centre, in a building opened in 1963 to commemorate what would have been Munch's 100th birthday. The collection consists of works and articles by Munch which he donated to the city of Oslo upon his death. The museum has in its permanent collection well over half of the entire production of his paintings and prints. This amounted to over 1200 paintings, 18000 prints, 500 plates, 2240 books, six sculptures and various other items. The museum also contained a conservation department. The original museum was designed by architects Fougner and Myklebust, with the latter playing an important role in the expansion and renovation of the museum in 1994, for the 50th anniversary of the death of Munch. It was here in 2004 that a version of The Scream painting was stolen. Within weeks of the theft the museum was opened after a $6.5 million security makeover. This included security barriers at the entrance to the museum, a museum which was less open plan, airport type security including x-ray machines and metal detection assets and further barriers which slow down any thief at the exit. The last exhibition at this original museum closed at the beginning of October 2021, whereupon the new museum opened at few weeks later.

Artist - Edvard Munch

Born in 1863, Munch was a Norwegian painter and his best known work The Scream has become an iconic image in the art world. In 1881 Munch enrolled at the Royal School of art and Design in Oslo. From a young age Munch was influenced by artists such as Edouard Manet and Vincent van Gogh and during these early years he experimented with many styles. Munch continued to employ a variety of brushstroke techniques and colour palettes throughout the 1880s and 1890s, as he struggled to define his style. Travel to Paris and Berlin brought new influences and outlets and his style would later come to be defined as humans and landscapes in simplified forms. With heavy outlines, sharp contrasts and much emotional content, which depicted a state of mind rather than external reality. In 1889 whilst he was in Paris, his father died leaving his family destitute. He returned home and arranged a large loan from a wealthy Norwegian collector, when family relatives failed to help, and so assumed financial responsibility for his family from then on.

As his fame and wealth grew his general health began to deteriorate and his emotional state had been and still was, insecure. A mental breakdown in 1908 forced him to give up heavy drinking but he was cheered by his increasing artistic acceptance by the people of Oslo, along with his increased exposure in the museums of his home city. His later years were spent working in peace and privacy, until the outbreak of World War I found him with divided loyalties as many of his friends were German. In the 1930s his German patrons, many Jewish, lost their fortunes and some their lives during the rise of the Nazi movement. Munch died in his house near Oslo in January 1944, a month after his 80th birthday, with his Nazi-orchestrated funeral suggesting to Norwegians that he had indeed been a Nazi sympathiser. Although his works were banned throughout Nazi occupied Europe most of them survived World War II, securing him a famous legacy.

Painting – The Scream(s)

This painting exists in four versions with the agonized face becoming one of the most iconic images in art, seen as symbolizing the anxiety of the human condition. Munch created two versions in paint and two in pastels between 1893 and 1910, but each version is still unique. They have rarely travelled or been exhibited outside Norway.

The Scream 1 - completed in 1893 and is pastel on cardboard. This earliest execution of The Scream appears to be the version in which Munch mapped out the essentials of the composition. It is part of the Munch Museum collection.

The Scream 2 - painted in 1893 and is oil, tempera (a permanent fast drying solution consisting of coloured pigments mixed with egg) and pastel on cardboard and is by far the best known version of The Scream. The painting is further unique because it has a tiny inscription, written in pencil, at the upper left corner of its frame which reads 'could only have been painted by a madman.' It was later confirmed as being the painters handwriting and is suggested he is alluding to his mental struggles. First exhibited in 1893, in a solo exhibition of his work in Berlin, it was purchased by the Norwegian industrialist Olaf Schou. He in turn donated the work to the National Gallery, Oslo, in 1910 and was also subject to theft in 1994 but later recovered.

The Scream 3 - the second pastel on cardboard version but created two years later and considered the most colourful and vibrant of the four versions. It is also further unique in that the frame was hand painted by the artist to include his poem detailing his inspiration for the work. To fit the space at the bottom of the frame, whilst preserving his line breaks, Munch recorded the poem in two columns of five and then three lines, separated by a vertical line.

I was walking along the road with two friends

The sun was setting – the sky turned blood-red.

And I felt a wave of Sadness – I paused

tired to Death – Above the blue-black

Fjord and City Blood and Flaming tongues hovered

My friends walked on – I stayed

behind – quaking with Angst – I

felt the great Scream in Nature

  This version was owned by the German Jewish art collector Hugo Simon a banker and politician. He was persecuted, plundered and forced into exile by the Nazis. He sold it to Norwegian businessman Thomas Olsen in 1937, with Olsen and Munch already acquaintances. During World War II just before the Nazi invasion of Norway, Olsen hid the painting in a barn to prevent it from falling into German hands. It remained in the Olsen family until 2012 when his son sold the work at Sotheby's for nearly $120 million. The buyer was reported to have been New York financier and art collector Leon Black.

ART CRIME AND SECURITY

The Scream 4 - painted in 1910 and is just tempera on cardboard. It was completed during a period when Munch revisited some of his prior compositions. It may have been created by Munch as a personal copy for him to keep after selling the more famous 1893 version. This version was stolen from the Munch Museum in 2004 and is the main subject matter of this chapter. It was only insured against damage, not theft, as the museum stated they could not afford the insurance against theft and in any case, much the same as the ISGM theft, the painting was irreplaceable.

The Scream following the expiration of its copyright, led to it acquiring further iconic status in popular culture. The mask worn by the primary antagonists of the Wes Craven Scream series of horror films is based on the painting. The principal alien antagonists named The Silence in the Dr Who television series, have an appearance partially based on The Scream and the characters known as the Men in Black, that became popular amongst UFO conspiracy theorists during the 1950s and 60s.

Persons of Interest

Although this chapter concentrates of the theft in 2004 of The Scream 4 from the Munch Museum, there has long been a suggested Norwegian organised crime link between this and the 1994 theft of The Scream 2. As a result, there are a number of persons of interest who overlap in relation to their alleged involvement, and the subsequent enquiries made during both investigations by the Norwegian police and other law enforcement agencies.

In the Oslo City Court on Tuesday 2nd May 2006 three of six men charged with the theft of The Scream, were found guilty and sentenced to prison terms of between four and eight years. Two of the men were also ordered to repay the city $121 million part of the insured value of the painting, which remained missing. If the painting were to be found, the repayment order would be withdrawn under Norwegian law. The prosecutor also offered to seek a lighter prison sentence in the appeal court for any of those convicted who then gave information leading the authorities to the missing art. Three initial acquittals reflected the gaps in the original police investigation but prosecutors in Norway have a right of appeal so none of the initial decisions would necessarily stand. The city had offered a reward of $323,000 for assistance leading to the recovery of the stolen painting.

Pal Enger

Four men were convicted of the 1994 theft and attempting to sell stolen property, The Scream 2. The team was led by Pal Enger who was sentenced to six years in prison. Enger was no stranger to art theft. He had already spent four years in prison in the late 1980s for the theft of another Munch artwork, The Vampire. After the 2004 theft, he told police he knew who committed the crime but was not prepared to name them as he believed there should be honour amongst thieves. He was never charged in relation to any of the events in 2004.

David Toska

Was heavily involved in organised crime and is believed to have ordered the theft to distract the authorities, law enforcement and the public from a serious armed cash robbery that had taken place four days earlier. He was never charged in relation to the theft but was strongly suspected to be one of the organisers.

Bjorn Hoen

The main organizer of the plot, he was convicted of procuring the Audi vehicle used in the theft and trying to negotiate the sale of the painting. In court prosecutors played tapes of a phone discussion relating to the painting, between Hoen and another defendant. He was sentenced to seven years in prison and ordered to pay half of the $121 million compensation order.

Petter Tharaldsen

A career criminal who the police accused of driving the getaway car, he was sentenced to eight years (but this was increased to nine after prosecutors appealed) in prison and ordered to pay the other half of the compensation order. An associate of Toska.

Stian Skjold

Stian Skjold the only defendant whom prosecutors had argued was one of the gunmen inside the museum. In his evidence Skjold denied any knowledge of the robbery but admitted that in September 2004 he transferred the paintings, stored in a rubbish bag, from a parked bus owned by another defendant to the boot of a car. Skjold further gave evidence that he had been hired to make the switch but that he did not know by whom and in the end, was never paid. Undercover investigators tailing Skjold witnessed the transfer, a few miles west of Oslo but failed to intervene in time to rescue the painting. He was initially acquitted but then sentenced by an appeal court to over five years the following year. The other gunman died of a heroin overdose later in 2004, the police later disclosed.

Petter Rosenvinge

Petter Rosenvinge discussed vague efforts to sell the painting with Hoen and as the former owner of the Audi was sentenced to over four years for supplying the getaway car to Hoen and participating in the plot. An associate of Toska who was a mechanic and familiar with firearms.

Thomas Nataas

A well-known professional drag racer, he was accused of hiding the pictures in a bus he owned and controlled for a month. Nataas acknowledged that the paintings had been stashed in his bus, on his land, after the robbery but said that they had been put there against his wishes. Tharaldsen had asked permission before the robbery to put something in the bus, Nataas said he had refused. He later said he found the painting in his bus but did not alert police because he feared for the safety of his family if he did so. The trial judge summarised in court that his actions were worthy of criticism but nonetheless, too passive to be punishable with a conviction and he was subsequently acquitted.

Theft

At about 11:00 hrs on Sunday 22nd August 2004 at the Munch Museum, with about seventy visitors already inside, a car pulled up alongside the main building. Two men got out of the car and ran towards the entrance of the museum. They wore hooded sweatshirts; gloves and their faces were covered. The men also brandished handguns. They had circumvented the main entrance and instead had entered via a set of doors adjacent to the café, which had been left open for visitor comfort. They then went past the main visitor desk whereupon staff pressed the panic button under the desk to alert police. The raiders then took the long route around the museum getting security staff to lay on the ground whilst they took away their radios. As they made their way across the far side of the museum where The Scream was located, they shouted and pointed their guns at visitors. When they reached the painting they ripped it from the wall. They ran back to their car and departed at great speed having stolen the painting in less than five minutes.

By 11:20 hrs Oslo Police were on the scene and they immediately cordoned off the area and had identified sixty plus witnesses. The getaway car had been noticed by other witnesses and identified as a black Audi with just the driver and police were given a partial number plate. Police immediately began a search for the vehicle which at that point proved to be their best lead. Some hours after the theft officers had traced the escape route taken by the raiders as they found broken pieces of the frame along stretches of different roads. As the raiders made their escape they were concerned the frame of the painting contained a tracking device and so began breaking it up and throwing it out the car window. Eventually, not far from the museum the getaway car was found abandoned. However, the raiders had cleverly covered the inside of the vehicle with fire extinguisher powder and therefore nullified any forensic opportunities for investigators. But in their haste to abandon the vehicle and transfer to another they left a handgun behind in the footwell of the vehicle, which would again prove a vital piece of evidence.

Within hours of the raid a detective in the Oslo police dealing with informants received a call from an angry Petter Rosenvinge. He advised the detective that he had recently prepared an Audi vehicle for a criminal associate and passed the vehicle over to him on the morning of the raid and that he had no idea it would be used for the theft. Once the Audi was confirmed as the same vehicle Rosenvinge not wishing to be implicated, offered up the names of Bjorn Hoen and Petter Tharaldsen to the detective.

As we know a decade earlier The Scream 2 had been stolen from the National Museum and investigators considered whether the two crimes may be linked. Police then spoke to Pal Enger who denied any involvement, neither was there any evidence that linked

Enger to this particular theft. He chose not to specifically name those who had committed the raid but offered to help negotiate its return. Police declined his offer.

Thomas Nataas, at some point, was approached by Petter Tharaldsen to store something on his bus but did not disclose the nature of the item. Natass refused the request but confirmed the bus was still located at his farm. Tharaldsen never asked him again and Natass thought nothing more of it. Natass was away in Germany drag racing when he received a call from Tharaldsen enquiring of his whereabouts. That same evening he saw news reports in his hotel room about the theft of The Scream and was immediately concerned about Tharaldsen and what might now be stored on his bus. On his return home he went onto the bus, which always remained unlocked but had not been used for three years. On entering the bus he could see the inside had been disturbed and upon lifting a bench cover saw the stolen Scream, which had been wrapped in a rubbish bag. He immediately contacted Tharaldsen and demanded he remove the painting but, as we know, did not alert the authorities.

During the investigation police were at a loss as to the real motive for the theft of such an iconic painting, that could never be sold on. Police thought the answer might lie in another more violently robbery, which had taken place four months previously and carried out by some of the most dangerous organised criminals in Norway. Stavanger is an important city situated on the Atlantic coast 150 miles from the capital Oslo and was the location for the raid by eleven heavily armed men wearing masks and body armour. They had arrived to raid the headquarters of Nokas, Norway's central cash services location and stole the equivalent of $2.5 million in cash. The robbery lasted fifteen minutes but police had already been alerted and arrived on scene before the robbers has made their escape. A shootout then ensued whereby a policeman was killed. Police believed that the organised crime group was led by David Toska and he had ordered the theft of The Scream to divert government and police resources away from the more lucrative Stavanger robbery. Crucial leads for investigators at this point were that that the gun found in the vehicle had been subject to a theft from a home near to where Petter Rosenvinge lived (albeit circumstantial) and CCTV from the Stavanger raid showed one of the robbers with another weapon, also stolen from the same home. Rosenvinge was now linked to the getaway car, the gun in the car and the Stavanger robbery. In addition to this money found in the home of Tharaldsen after his arrest was forensically found to have a dust covering of glass, linking it to the Stavanger robbery. Cash with which police believed he was paid with for his involvement in The Scream.

Police by now had a number of suspects under surveillance, implicated in both the museum and Stavanger crimes and Rosenvinge was central to both enquiries. The officer dealing with Rosenvinge as a long term informant, was advised of the evidence by investigating officers and as a result let Rosenvinge know that their relationship was at an end. Whilst on the brink of arresting suspects, police were no nearer to finding The Scream, which was actually still hidden away on the bus. The thieves now anxious to move the painting before police moved in on them, contacted Nataas. The police begun conducting phone taps of the suspects the previous day so operationally were unprepared for when the painting was transferred from the bus. Stian Skjold one of the gunmen from the museum was believed to have driven a Mercedes car to the farm and later admitted this in evidence, to collect and transfer The Scream to a safer place. But for a number of reasons police did not manage to intervene and secure the painting. This Mercedes was later found by another surveillance team outside the home of the fiancée of David Toska, the trail for the painting had gone cold again. Eight months after the theft, police and prosecutors began plans to arrest the suspects in the hope of breaking up the crime ring and recovering the painting. Rosenvinge was the first to be arrested, then Tharaldsen was brought into custody from a prison he was already in and then the planner Bjorn Hoen. David Toska was then tracked down and arrested in Spain, but no charges were subsequently brought in relation to The Scream.

    The prison sentences and the fines were believed to have perhaps concentrated the minds of those involved in Norwegian organised crime. In a development that came as a surprise to the Norwegian public and those in the art world in August 2006, police recovered The Scream. They would not disclose how, when or why this recovery was secured or brokered. What seemed more important to the Norwegian government and law enforcement was that the famous painting was now safely back in the Munch Museum.

Chapter 4
Peru

Archaeological Site – La Mina

The site in the Jequetepeque Valley on the northern coast of Peru, 400 miles north of the capital Lima, was looted so much by the Peruvian people themselves in 1988, that it almost disappeared. The site of the tomb of the Lord of La Mina a ruler of the ancient Moche Culture, is set in an area which is vast, bleak and gives away no sign of the tomb below. This has been exacerbated, in the case of the Moche Culture, because of the excellent preservation qualities of the area, that much of coastal Peru is dry with organic minerals found at many sites and because Moche metalworkers were quite skilled in working with gold. The tomb was discovered by a local goat herder, before word spread and the serious looters moved in. This was unfortunately sometime before archaeologists were notified, who could secure the site and the looters subsequently took priceless ceramic figures and bowls. When archaeologist did arrive they were met with devastation of the tomb, with copious fragments of smaller antiquities scattered around, the tomb almost completely looted.

The Moche were one of the great early civilisations in South America, with a system of kingdoms ruled by lords within a greater valley network. Moche Culture has only really been discovered in recent decades as a result of various finds in Peru. But looting of this particular site has been described, embarrassingly for the

Peruvian authorities, as that on the scale of anything previously undertaken by the conquistadors. With no written language, everything the archaeologist knows about the Moche Culture comes from their art. It was a society based on religion, warfare and ceremonial rituals. Their art specialised not only in painted ceramics but also metals, such as gold. The tomb of the Lord of La Mina, much like in Egypt, contained a mummified body surrounded by a selection of magnificent artworks and at its centre a golden Octopoid Headdress. In the months after the looting there was no trace of the priceless objects and in particular, no leads as to who might now be in possession of the centrepiece headdress.

Antiquity - Octopoid Headdress

The looters and those involved in the fencing of the headdress must have soon realised its worth on the international antiquities market. Referred to as the Moche Mona Lisa it is one of the most famous looted Peruvian antiquities. The 1300 year old embossed gold headdress described as a sea god or goddess, is an octopoid creature with a human/feline face in the centre with blue eye stones and tiger type teeth showing elongated fangs. Eight curving tentacles along which are embossed numerous triangles suggesting a scaly surface, The ends of the tentacles suggest mouths similar to serpents often found protruding from figures in Moche artwork. It had an estimated worth on the antiquities market of close to $2 million, when it was rescued.

Persons of Interest

Raul Apesteguia

A Peruvian national and based in Lima, he was a high profile buyer of Peruvian art and owned an immense private collection. He was a consultant to collectors, others involved in the study of art and moved within influential circles of people in Peru, where he was well respected. However, he did have a less then unblemished past. In the 1970s he was caught with a team of looters in the Nazca region of Peru and served a short prison sentence. It was believed he had information regarding the looted art from La Mina, although he was never implicated by police. It has been suggested that after looting, a local antiquities trafficker acquired the headdress and then, acting as the fence, sold it to Apesteguia. He could then use his international contacts to sell it on for greater profit. In 1992 four years after the looting, images of the headdress appeared for the first time. A book called Gold from Ancient Peru was published and on its cover was the octopoid headdress, with Apesteguia listed as one of the books contributors. In 1995 a second book was published containing more pictures of the headdress and once again Apesteguia was a contributor. In 1996 two unknown men forced their way into his Lima apartment, which was then ransacked and Apesteguia murdered. Publicly there was no obvious motive for the attack but many suggested a connection with the octopoid headdress. The murder remains unsolved to this day.

Leonardo Patterson

Patterson is a controversial antiquities dealer who specialises in works from Central and South America. Raised in Costa Rica, he started his career as an apprentice jeweller moving on to work as an antiquities broker as he gained exposure to a wider range of objects, until finally graduating to the role of international dealer and collector. Patterson began to deal on a large scale in New York in the 1960s but at a time when restrictions on the trade of antiquities were loose. When restrictions tightened in the 1970s on the export of antiquities his activities in this areas faced a setback. In 1984 Patterson was charged by the FBI with wire fraud as part of an attempt to sell a fake Fresco from the Maya Civilisation period to an art dealer and he was sentenced to probation. In 1995 he was appointed as cultural attaché to the United Nations. Administrators at the UN had not conducted due diligence before his was put in post and subsequent questions about his past then caused him to resign. He then began to spend more time in Europe, particularly Germany. In 1997 an extensive book was published on ancient art from the Americas and it too featured the octopoid headdress. This publication had been put together by Patterson.

Theft

In 2000 art collector and former antiquities smuggler, turned police informant, Michel van Rijn who has worked with law enforcement agencies across the world to facilitate locating and repatriating looted antiquities, saw the headdress in the book published by Patterson and knew it was looted. He then began an extensive and relentless internet campaign against Patterson, relating to the book and the headdress, which not only highlighted its history but also the connection Patterson had with the antiquity. It was personally and professionally damaging for Patterson connecting his name with suspected looted antiquities. Although he made no personal reply to van Rijn, Patterson then instructed a London lawyer to respond to these allegations. The lawyer for Patterson suggested that van Rijn had got his facts wrong and that ownership of the headdress, in the 1997 publication, had been wrongly attributed to Patterson and was actually the property of another private collector. Patterson therefore denied any wrongdoing via his lawyer, whilst threatening legal action against van Rijn and then mistakenly assumed the matter was at an end. Van Rijn was by now visiting Lima and had contacted the Peruvian authorities, their law enforcement agencies, the head of Interpol in Peru and along with a Peruvian art expert tried to persuade them to start a full investigating. This proved fruitless so van Rijn continued with his personal internet campaign, which he had by now intensified and the allegations became deeply unpleasant for Patterson, both personally and professionally.

In 2004 through his lawyer Patterson issued a writ to gag order. An order which effectively orders an individual or organisation to refrain from publishing, making available or otherwise putting out any statements of a defamatory nature about Patterson. In particular that he may be an art thief. An injunction was subsequently issued by the courts, however, van Rijn ignored both the order and the injunction and undeterred continued with his campaign. With the legal options ineffective Patterson eventually contacted van Rijn personally to strike a deal. Van Rijn informed Patterson the only way forward was to present the octopoid headdress, so it could then be returned to Peru and he would then close down the campaign against him. Patterson later attended a meeting with van Rijn in London whereupon he produced the headdress, which he alleged he had spent time tracking down and procuring from another source, utilising his vast network of art contacts.

In July 2006 Patterson attended the London office of his lawyers in possession of the headdress, where van Rijn was also present with his lawyer and the headdress was then shown to all. Before the meeting ended Patterson produced a document which claimed to prove the provenance of the headdress. This document showed the headdress had been purchased in 1987 from Raul Apesteguia, by Everet Rassiger and imported into Germany via Frankfurt with the assistance of Romero Passeo. All three of these men were now dead. It also stated Rassiger then sold on the headdress to another collector in Munich for $18000. The document was signed by a Jack Franklin. Van Rijn was not convinced about the authenticity of the document and made that clear. The headdress was then left in the custody of the London lawyer, whilst final negotiations continued.

Not prepared to take any chances and knowing that both Patterson and the headdress were in London, van Rijn contacted the London Metropolitan Police, making them aware of the location of the stolen antiquity belonging to Peru. However, neither the London police nor Interpol could act until Peruvian authorities could indeed confirm it had been looted from La Mina. This was eventually confirmed by an archaeologist to the Peruvian police, who then contacted their counterparts in London. Concerned the headdress may again disappear along with Patterson, London police waited anxiously for confirmation from Peru. With that confirmation received soon after, police instigated activity from undercover officers who attended the premises of the lawyer and effectively seized the headdress as a stolen antiquity, requiring restoration to the Peruvian authorities. The lawyer then informed his client Patterson of those events.

Despite its restoration, there were still unanswered questions about the headdress, that had been left unresolved by the apparently fake provenance document previously produced by Patterson in the lawyers London office. A second document was later received by the London lawyer from Patterson in Germany. It stated that Patterson had acquired the headdress from a fellow collector in Munich called Anton Roeckl. Advising his lawyer that he had obtained it from Roeckl for the sole purpose of bringing it to London, to hand over to van Rijn. Roeckl himself stated in the documents that he purchased the headdress from Raul Apesteguia and had it shipped to Germany, whereupon it was authenticated before being sold. It had therefore been in his possession up until its sale to Patterson. His name also appeared in the book published in 1997 by Patterson. At the end of 2006 the headdress was flown back to Peru and it now resides in the National Museum in Lima as a national icon, under tight security.

Chapter 5
Austria

Museum – Belvedere

The museum is located in a historic building complex in Vienna consisting of two palaces, the Upper and Lower Belvedere, as well as an Orangery and palace stables. The buildings are set in a park landscape on the south-eastern edge of the city centre and built as a summer residence for Prince Eugene, who was also an art collector. He was a field marshal in the army of the Holy Roman Empire of the Austrian Hasburg dynasty, a monarchy ruling over a multinational state, during the 17th and 18th centuries. He was one of the most successful military commanders of his time and rose to the highest offices of state at the Imperial court in Vienna. Despite the title, he was effectively a military commander and a politician who chose his own allegiances and was a successful and influential figure across Europe.

In 1697 he purchased a sizable plot of land and plans for the actual Belvedere garden complex were drawn up by an Austrian architect, with military engineer Johann von Hildebrandt commissioned to oversee the build. Construction on the smaller Lower Belvedere started in 1712 and was completed around 1717 whereupon construction on the larger Upper Belvedere then began. Despite some structural problems and extensive interior design, the Upper building was completed by 1723. When Prince Eugene died in his smaller city palace in April 1736, he did not leave a legally binding will. At this point his only heir, his niece Victoria, moved into the Belvedere. She immediately made it clear that she aimed to auction off the palace complex as soon as possible. However, after an unsuccessful marriage and a return to her home city of Turin did she decide to sell, some eight years later. The Belvedere and some of the art collection of Prince Eugene was purchased from her by Maria Theresa, the daughter of the Charles VI, ruler of the Hasburg dynasty. The complex was somewhat eclipsed by the other imperial palaces, and at first the buildings were left unused.

From 1871 various parts of the imperial art collection were placed on display at the Belvedere. In 1903 a state sponsored gallery was opened in the Lower Belvedere. Later in 1921 the palace, now virtually in full use as a museum, was renamed the Austrian Gallery Belvedere. It came to comprise the Baroque Museum in the Lower Belvedere opened in 1923, the Gallery of 19th Century Art at the Upper Belvedere from 1924 and the Modern Gallery at the Orangery from 1929. During the war years the Belvedere, as a result of the Nazi annexation of Austria, came under their administration and sole authority. This was a similar story across Germany and other European nations invaded by the Nazi regime. In 1955, after years of rebuilding and renovation works, the Upper Belvedere was reopened to the public showing works by Gustav Klimt, Egon Schiele and other major Austrian artists. Today the Belvedere houses the greatest collection of Austrian art dating from the Middle Ages to the present day and this is complemented by the works of other international artists. It presents an almost complete overview of the development of art in the country and an insight into Austrian history. The largest collection of paintings in the world by Gustav Klimt lies at the heart of the Belvedere, with paintings such as Judith and the Head of Holofernes completed in 1901 and The Kiss completed in 1908.

In relation to the looting of art during World War II and the subsequent restitution of paintings to their rightful owners or heirs, the Belvedere has not been without controversy. The theft of art by the Nazi regime will be the subject of later chapters. This chapter is concerned with the theft of one of those paintings the Woman in Gold. But to put this in context it is worth noting here that the Allied Forces returned stolen art, in the first instance, to their country of origin. This system was then reliant upon those nations to facilitate restitution of the art back to their citizens, but this did not always happen and the Belvedere were at the forefront of a number of subsequent litigations.

In 1959, holocaust survivor Alice Morgenstern whose husband was murdered in Auschwitz, filed a claim to the Austrian authorities. She stated that the picture, Four Trees by Austrian artist Egon Schiele, which used to be owned by them, was now hanging in the Upper Belvedere. She further alleged that they had never sold the painting but gave it their friend and Vienna lawyer, Robert Rohrl, for safekeeping before annexation with Germany and he subsequently died. In March 2020 the Austrian Advisory Commission recommended that the Schiele be restituted to Morgenstern's heirs. In November 2006 after more than five decades of legal disputes, a panel ruled that the Edvard Munch painting Summer Night at the Beach on display at the Belvedere, was to be returned to Marina Fistoulari-Mahler. She was the granddaughter and sole heir of Alma Mahler, wife of Austrian composer Gustav Mahler. In 2014 the Belvedere was ordered to restitute the Farmer's Kitchen / Kitchen Interior painting by Wilhelm Leibl to the heirs of Martha Liebermann, the widow of German artist Max Liebermann.

FIVE FAMOUS THEFTS

Artist – Gustav Klimt

Klimt born in 1862, was an Austrian born artist known for his paintings, murals and sketches and showed early artistic talent. His primary subject came to be the female body with many of his works marked by an unapologetic eroticism. He was prominent member of the Austrian Succession art movement from 1897, that was closely related to Art Nouveau. This was an art genre that was inspired by particular artistic ways of working such as natural forms, dynamism, movement, asymmetry. As well as the use of modern materials such as iron, gold, glass and ceramics. As his own personal style developed he achieved new success with the paintings of his so called golden phase, many of which included gold leaf finishing. Klimt travelled very little, but trips to Italy famous for their beautiful mosaics, are said to have most likely inspired his gold technique. These works brought positive critical reaction and financial success. However, he avoided cafe society and seldom socialized with other artists of the time. His eventual fame usually brought wealthy high end patrons to his door and he could even afford to be highly selective. His painting method for the lengthy sittings he required were very deliberate. Rumour was that things sometimes went further and although he was very active sexually, kept his affairs discreet and avoided personal scandal. Klimt died in 1918, having suffered a stroke and pneumonia and was buried in Vienna. Numerous paintings by him were left unfinished.

Painting - Portrait of Adele Bloch-Bauer I aka Woman in Gold/ Lady in Gold

Completed between 1903 and 1907 the portrait was commissioned by the husband of Adele, Ferdinand, who was a wealthy Jewish banker and sugar producer. The painting was seized by the Nazis in 1941 and allocated for display at the Belvedere. The portrait is the final and most fully representative work of his golden phase and was the first of two depictions of Adele by Klimt. These were two of several works by the artist that the family owned. Ferdinand Bloch-Bauer commissioned Klimt to paint the portrait of his wife and Klimt proceeded to draw over a hundred preparatory sketches. Undertaking more extensive preparations for the portrait than any other piece he ever worked on. The portrait shows Adele sitting on a golden throne type chair, with a jewelled choker around her neck, in front of a golden starry background. The painting is composed of oil on canvas with silver and copious gold overlay. Much of the work is by an elaborate technique of using silver and gold leaf carefully overlaid in particular areas. Then by adding varying decorative motifs with a paint mixture consisting of a binder. The frame for the painting, also covered in gold leaf, was made by the Austrian architect Josef Hoffman. In June 2006 the painting was sold to Ronald Lauder son of Estee and chairman emeritus of the Estee Lauder Company, for $135 million. Lauder then placed the work in the Neue Gallery, a New York based public gallery he co-founded. The painting has been on display at the location ever since. In 2015 the painting and the story of its theft and later recovery, was the subject of the film Woman in Gold. Starring Helen Mirren as the niece of Adele, Maria Altmann, and Ryan Reynolds as her lawyer.

Theft

For a number of years after its completion the Woman in Gold, along with other commissioned paintings by Gustav Klimt, hung in the house of Adele and Ferdinand Bloch-Bauer on Elisabethstrasse, Vienna. But in January 1925 Adele died of a brain disease after a very short illness, at the age of only forty-three. Ferdinand was heartbroken and left his wife's room just as it was when she died. Ferdinand then went about converting her room into an almost memorial room and it displayed all the Klimt paintings, including the Woman in Gold. Adele had made clear in her will what she wanted to happen to the Klimt paintings. Her wish was to leave her two portraits and four landscapes by Klimt to the Belvedere. But at this point the paintings remained in the memorial bedroom of Adele.

During the 1930s the Nazi regime came to power and as their territorial ambitions became clear, Ferdinand foresaw the Nazis strategic intention to invade Austria. In 1938 Hitler ordered the annexation of Austria and the German army marched into Vienna, unopposed. Before they arrived and set up their administrative logistics, Ferdinand had fled the capital to his country residence, across the border in Czechoslovakia. With time to escape at a premium Ferdinand left behind the Woman in Gold hanging on the wall in the room of Adele, as well as other valuable art. As he left the house for the last time under cover of darkness, he walked past the Academy of Fine Arts in Vienna. Ironically, the academy which had rejected Hitler who had applied there for a place to study in 1907. The very year Klimt finished painting the Woman in Gold. Ferdinand subsequently died penniless in Switzerland in 1945.

With the arrival of the Nazi regime to the streets of Vienna, came fear for their own existence from the Jewish community. Whether it be daily persecution on the streets of Vienna, high taxation or outright theft and seizure of their property and assets. One night Gestapo agents attended the address of Maria Altmann, the niece of Adele, and her parents. They asked for jewellery which Maria had not long been given by Ferdinand as a wedding gift in 1937. It was an exquisite diamond necklace, with matching earrings, which had belonged to Adele. Again, ironically, these were subsequently given to the wife of Hermann Goering which she went on to wear publicly.

These were dangerous times for the rest of the Bloch-Bauer extended family. Maria's husband, Fritz, was then imprisoned in

Dachau concentration camp until the family had officially signed over property to the Nazis. Fritz was subsequently released when another family member signed over a factory asset to the Nazis. Fritz returned home, clearly having been mistreated whereupon he and Maria, now fearing for their lives, wasted no time in planning their escape from Austria. They managed to escape across the border into the Netherlands with the help of a German farmer. Once the Nazis had secured the Bloch-Bauer factory they turned their attention to Ferdinand's entire art collection. They claimed Ferdinand owed huge amounts of taxes and sent a Gestapo agent to the house on Elisabethstrasse to seek payment via art assets. The agent was seemingly conversant with the art collection of Ferdinand and organised the removal of certain paintings that he knew Hitler and Goering would like. The agent knew that the arguably decadent Klimt portraits would not be of interest to the Nazi elite, so decided to keep them and sell them off. Also in the house was a famous Stradivarius cello lent to the family by the Rothschild family, this was also taken and returned by the German authorities in 1956. Gustav Bloch-Bauer, Maria's father died two weeks after the Gestapo raided their family home.

The Gestapo agent, portrayed in the 2015 film as Felix Landau an agent assigned to oversee the wealth of the Bloch-Bauer family, sold off the Klimt paintings and the Woman in Gold that then ended up in the Belvedere. However, other sources state that German attorney Friedrich Fuhrer administered their sale on behalf of the Nazi regime and in 1941 the Austrian State Gallery acquired the Klimt paintings.

Importantly, in 1945, the year of his death, Ferdinand rewrote his will in which he left his entire estate to his nieces and nephews although he made no reference to the Woman in Gold, which he assumed was lost forever. The Belvedere from this point on claimed ownership of the painting as they had legitimately purchased them from Felix Landau and because Adele had set out a wish in her will that the painting should go to the Belvedere, despite the subsequent will made by Ferdinand with no mention of the painting. As the painting was of a Jewish woman displayed in a museum during a Nazi occupation the painting became known as the Lady in Gold or the Woman in Gold. At the end of the war the Allied Forces charged countries with the return of stolen paintings to individual citizens of the relevant countries, therefore the rest of the Klimt paintings were returned to the Belvedere where they all stayed for many years. With no ensuing claims of ownership but more importantly, no restitution attempts made by the Belvedere.

Some years later Maria and Fritz moved to the United States, settling in Los Angeles. They lived in a modest apartment and Maria began a clothing business. But everything changed in 1998. The Museum of Modern Art in New York loaned some paintings from an Austrian gallery by Egon Schiele. His heirs claimed the paintings had been looted by the Nazis and after the loan of the works was completed, they were impounded by the US courts before they could leave for Austria. The case made Maria think about the Klimt paintings and decided it was time to contact a lawyer, as she believed there was not any actual evidential proof they belonged to the Belvedere. She then contacted her nephew Randol Schoenberg who was working for a large New York law firm at that time. He subsequently left the firm to work solely on the Klimt case as like Maria, his family had holocaust connections.

From a legal perspective, at this point, they knew that Adele had stated in her will in 1925 that the Woman in Gold along with other Klimt paintings were to be left to the Belvedere. So when legal claim enquiries were made with the Belvedere, convinced its museum contained no looted art, it opened its archives for examination to prove it. A journalist interested in the whole subject matter of Nazi art activities, Hubertus Czernin, then spent a whole year in those archives conducting research. He discovered key documents, as well secretly looking at other literature he was not authorised to view, but still had access to. They showed the Belvedere were themselves not completely sure of ownership. Alluding to the fact that they should ideally have had a signed document from Ferdinand Bloch-Bauer authorising their ownership. His research also found that although Adele had left the paintings to the Belvedere, Ferdinand had overruled that request. He had been the person who had paid for the portraits and his last will had explicitly stated that all previous testaments relating to the Klimt paintings were to be null and void. His will stated everything should be left to Maria, her sister and brother.

As a result of these developments, the Austrian Culture Minister, unsurprisingly, closed these archives immediately and announced the setting up of a government committee on the ownership of the Klimt paintings, primarily the Woman in Gold. Ultimately the committee worked to stifle any attempts for Maria to make claim to the painting. After the committee decided during initial arbitration that the painting should not be returned, in order to sue in Austria, Maria was required to put down a large deposit reflecting the value of the paintings. In this case it would have been several million dollars for Maria just to initiate a lawsuit. Randol decided instead to try and sue Austria in the US courts. He filed his complaint against Austria in August 2000 based on copyright law, in that Austria had made money in the US on sales of posters and books featuring the Klimt paintings.

After the lawsuit climbed several stages in the hierarchy of the US legal system, the US Supreme Court finally cleared the way for Maria to sue the Austrian government. In order to avoid a lengthy and expensive court battle, she agreed to binding arbitration in Austria. After some 'refocussing' by the Austrian authorities, thereby entering into a second arbitration in Austria, they finally agreed to return the Woman in Gold. This was in part because Randol had convinced her that arbitration was the best choice, given that she might not live to see the end of a lengthy court battle. She was after all over eighty years old when she first contacted him. After four months of binding arbitration in Austria, she and the other heirs were awarded five of the six paintings that had been stolen from her family by the Nazis. With three Austrian judges unanimously voting for something which their government was, in reality, totally opposed to. The fight to reclaim the Woman in Gold lasted approximately eight years.

ART CRIME

Chapter 1
Select Ancient Civilisations and Biblical Timeline

The most appropriate starting point for this book is a selected summary of ancient and biblical history, essentially where all art and antiquities began. There will not be extensive detail here, as I seek to keep the reader on track and give an overview that helps put artwork into an historical context. For that, there is a need to go back to the very beginning in relation to four important, but distinct elements. Prehistory, recorded history, ancient civilisations and the biblical timeline. So to better understand art, there is a need to have a basic grasp of its journey.

Prehistory can refer to the huge span of time since human life appeared on earth. The end of prehistory is typically defined as the start of written historical records, which covers 5000BC to the present day. The actual date can vary widely from geographical region to region, depending on the date when relevant records become a useful academic resource. The earliest written documents date back to the earliest civilization in today's Middle East.

For an ancient civilisation to be deemed as such, certain basic criteria have always been met. The civilisation should be made up of 10000 people or more, they would typically have settled by rivers and would have developed some kind of language be it spoken, written or both. They would then build cities, have a social order and engage in economics, farming, trade and most

ART CRIME AND SECURITY

importantly indulge in arts and crafts. The history of ancient civilisations usually covers the period of 3000BC to 500AD.

Select Ancient Civilisations (descending order)

3500BC Sumer – Middle East

The first universally agreed advanced civilisation meeting all the above criteria. It covered an area called Mesopotamia, that is in modern day Iraq and situated between the rivers of Tigris and Euphrates. Its language was Sumerian and the culture used logos and symbols.

3000BC Egyptian – Middle East (see following pages)

2500BC Indus – India

This civilisation spanned an area stretching from today's northeast Afghanistan, through much of Pakistan and into western and north-western India. It was concentrated around the Indus River.

2000BC China – Far East

China is among the world's oldest civilisations and in ancient times was ruled by three dynasties. The Xia dynasty was the first Chinese dynasty, but there is a severe lack of documented evidence about this dynasty. Antiquities however have been discovered and the dynasty is best known for its bronze making. They were followed by the Shang dynasty who ruled in the Yellow River valley commonly held to be the cradle of Chinese civilization. They were followed by the Zhou dynasty, the third and final ancient Chinese dynasty, before the beginning of Imperial China and many more dynasties.

2000BC Greek - Europe

1000BC Andean – South America (see following pages)

500AD Rome – Europe

The timelines of Egypt and Peru are further selected as they provide both for classic architecture and antiquity importance.

Egypt

Egypt has furnished the modern world with numerous high quality ancient antiquities and were one of the most advanced civilisations in terms of art.

3400BC – the earliest hieroglyphs were used as part of a formal writing system. Hieroglyphs combined logos, symbols and the alphabet to create some 1000 distinct written or drawn characters

3100BC – Egypt has single ruler for first time King Narmer

Pharaohs were the heads of state and religious leaders of Egypt and considered the divine intermediary between the gods and Egyptians. Pharaoh means 'Great House' a reference to the palaces in which they resided. Early rulers were called Kings, but the term pharaoh stuck due to popular culture. They were mainly male rulers but some were female, such as Queen Cleopatra. After death they were entombed and surrounded by riches to use in the afterlife, which was so important to them.

2600BC – construction starts on the Great Pyramid at Giza

1333BC – Tutankhamun rules from age nine or ten years and that rule ends when he dies ten years later

279BC – Ramesses rules during the biblical time of the Exodus

51BC – Queen Cleopatra in power

30BC – Battle of Actium, Egypt loses the battle and joins the Roman Empire. Antony and Cleopatra commit suicide

Peru (Andean)

1000BC – Chauvin Culture

100BC – 700AD Moche Culture known for its Moche gold

100BC – 700AD Nazca Culture known for the Nazca lines

1438 – 1532AD Inca Empire known for the Machu Picchu citadel

1532AD – Conquistadors arrive from Spain and wipe out the last ancient civilisations of not just Peru, but the whole of South America.

Nazca Culture

The Nazca Culture existed in a small coastal area of Peru and the culture produced an array of textiles and ceramics. The culture is famous for the Nazca lines, large motifs that can only be seen properly from the sky. They were created in the Nazca desert by way of incisions in the desert floor leaving different coloured soil exposed. Motifs include a hummingbird, a spider, a condor and a monkey. There is a belief by archaeologists that the lines were created so they could be seen by the gods in the sky.

Thirty miles south of the city of Nazca is the Chauchilla Cemetery. It contained mummified human remains and antiquities prior to the conquistadors, which are important as a source of archaeology for the Nazca culture. The cemetery had previously been looted extensively with human bones and pottery scattered around the area.

Select Biblical timeline (descending order)

A religious or cultural antiquity is an object that can have religious, cultural or personal significance. All religious traditions have objects that are used in worship or as a key symbol to followers of their beliefs, their traditions and their identity. They can be a means of signifying someone or something special, a visible link to its history, or as a sign of commitment and faith by its followers. Many antiquities are not always linked to specific religions but also to other groups and cultural traditions.

c4000BC – Genesis

Creation, Garden of Eden, Noah's Ark

c2090BC – Abraham

The journey to Canaan, a new nations calling, the father of the three faiths

c1890BC – Joseph

A coat of many colours, a slave in Egypt, a reversal of fortune, he is made a high administrator to the Pharaoh

c1525BC – Moses

As a baby in a basket, the burning bush, the ten commandments, Ark of the Covenant

c1446BC – The Exodus

Route of exodus, the seven plagues, parting of the red sea, bread falls from heaven

1406BC – Settlement in the Promised Land

Joshua succeeds Moses, fall of the Walls of Jericho, rise of the Philistines

c1075BC – Samson and Delilah

Delilah is a philistine and part of a plot, becomes lover to Samson, cuts his hair

c1043BC – David and Goliath

Saul first King of Israel. David a military hero defeats Goliath with the sling and a stone

1003BC – Kingdom of David

David becomes king, Jerusalem becomes capital, son Solomon succeeds

c966BC – Temple of Solomon

Organises country, discovery of gold, builds temple, the Ark placed in temple.

c900BC – Assyrian Era

Rise of invincible military power, first real use of a siege engine.

600BC – Persian Era

Cyrus the Great, Israel and Judah unified, Temple of Solomon rebuilt.

c33BC – Kingdom of Herod

Roman ruler of the region, ruled ruthlessly but carefully, expanded the Second Temple.

c4BC – Birth of Jesus

Prophesy and miraculous signs, immaculate conception, born in Bethlehem like King David, grows up in Nazareth.

28AD – John the Baptist

    Dissident figure against Pontius Pilate who hated Jews and was an apocalyptic prophet. Jesus baptised by John in River Jordan and a dove appears, Jesus has role as a healer and followed by Mary Magdalene. The passion of Jesus is to take his messages to Jerusalem.

30AD – The Passover

Passover events in Jerusalem, presence of money changers in temple angers Jesus. His action lead the temples high priest to seek his death. Judas betrays Jesus on the Mount of Olives and he is tried in the palace by Pontius Pilate. The road to Calvary, Jesus is stabbed by Roman Centurion Longinus after he is nailed to the crucifix to make sure he is dead, by a lance now known as the Spear of Destiny.

    From these key timelines connections can be made with famous architecture, antiquities and art that survive to this day. Some of the ancient antiquities will be referenced, including some of those that are fictitiously famous in popular culture in later chapters. As well as those that have connections to modern art, that tell religious stories by way of their important biblical depictions.

Chapter 2
Select Art Movements, Techniques, Architecture and Art

The following three lists allow for a snapshot of their most important parts. The art world has been divided up into an extensive number of art movements by history of art experts. This helps the student depict a common style within the artwork, or a particular group of artists, during that specific period of time. Importantly, this ties in with the common techniques used and although the changes in technique do not always run parallel with changes in the movement, they are always a good visual indicator of basic timescales. This is more so in modern art than antiquity. For simplicity a prominent artist will be listed in both the timeline and technique lists in relation to paintings.

Select Art Movements

Prehistoric c50000 – 250BC

Prehistoric art describes a broad range of art made by illiterate cultures, including some of the earliest human antiquities. Most accepted theories are that the art is part of religious rituals. Possibly to evoke hunting success.

Ancient Greek and Roman   650BC – 476AD

Through meticulous proportion and a focus on aesthetics, ancient Greek and Roman art became the foundation and inspiration of all western art. Among the techniques they perfected include methods of carving and casting sculpture, fresco paintings and constructing magnificent buildings.

Byzantine 476 – 1453   Artist: Duccio

From c300AD, as Christianity spread and became a legal religion, the Roman Emperor Constantine transferred the capital of his empire from Rome to Byzantium, renaming it Constantinople (Istanbul.) The term Byzantine describes art of the eastern Roman Empire and was concerned with representing the divine with the conveyance of power and mystery.

Renaissance 1430 – 1550   Artist: Sandro Botticelli

An era of new interest in learning as well as the development of arts. With new technologies and techniques including the discovery of linear perspective, the printing press, production of lead pencils and the use of oil paint. Throughout the 15th century, Florence was considered the cradle of the Renaissance and the most productive centre of art in Italy.

High Renaissance 1490 – 1530   Artist: Leonardo da Vinci

As Papal power stabilized in Rome, several popes commissioned art and architecture. Artists could access highly developed techniques of atmospheric perspective and many artists had sophisticated knowledge of anatomy and skills in the use of materials.

Dutch Golden Age 1585 – 1700   Artist: Jan Vermeer

Religion and political unrest had divided the Low Countries and the new Dutch Republic became the most prosperous nation in Europe. The church became a much less important artistic subject, with images of everyday people becoming the vogue. Still life, landscapes and interiors expressed the renewed interest in ordinary things.

Baroque 1600 – 1750 Artist: Rembrandt

The name is said to derive from the Portuguese word for a miss shaped pearl. Baroque art both embraced and developed High renaissance religious art, with an emphasis on landscapes. New techniques of light and dark were developed to create atmosphere, spectacle, illusion and grandeur.

Impressionism 1865 – 1885 Artist: Claude Monet

Primarily undertaken by Paris based artists, they used sketchy painting techniques and new materials. There subjects were landscapes and everyday people. They painted in rapid broken brush marks, in dabs of colour which seem to distort as the viewer moves closer and reform as they move away. The artists often painted in the open air directly in front of the subject matter.

Cubism 1907 – 1914 Artist: Pablo Picasso

Probably the most important and most influential modern art period, Cubism was actually created by Pablo Picasso and Georges Braque. The paintings depict their subject matter from different angles and as such look like little cubes inspiring the name Cubism. It became well known during World War II, as the Nazi leadership considered it to be degenerate art and was thus stolen and treated as such. Cubism abandons the perspective of space and the realistic modelling of figures that had been used since the Renaissance period.

Pop Art 1955 – 1970 Artist: Andy Warhol

From 1950s consumerism and as mass media surged, Pop Art developed in New York. This, along with mass-produced goods and mass-entertainment became known as popular culture. Pop artists produced colourful images based on film stars, comic strips, flags, packaging and food. Like pop music, its emphasis was largely on a celebration of a new modern world and newly empowered generation, but it had political aspects too.

Select Techniques

Clay

The most commonly used modelling material, clay is found throughout the world and has been used by artists since antiquity. The technique of hardening clay objects in a fire has been practised for about 30000 years. Early civilisations in the Middle East and China created clay sculpture and pottery. Many of the oldest antiquities found have survived, because they are made from clay and because of its ability to survive intense heat which just makes the substance harder.

Ceramics

Ceramics are objects made from clay by shaping, heating, glazing and then reheating to finish. The word ceramic derives from the Greek word keramos meaning potters clay. Like clay artefacts some ceramics are all that remain of some ancient cultures. Porcelain, for example, is different because of the clay used to make it and the temperatures used to heat it.

Marble

The smoothness and durability of marble and the ability of Greek sculptors made marble a particularly effective medium for the portrayal of human flesh. A type of calcium carbonate, when it is first quarried marble is soft and easy to work with but hardens over time and can be susceptible to cracking.

Mosaics

Created during the Byzantine era it is made by setting small pieces of glass or stone in cement or plaster. Mosaics decorated Greek and Roman floors and as religion became more accepted, mosaics were increasingly made to adorn church walls. The finest mosaics were created as shimmering wall mosaics, using gold, silver and coloured glass backed with metallic foil. The finest Byzantine mosaics were created for churches in Constantinople.

Fresco - Michelangelo

A method of painting with water-based pigments on freshly plastered walls or ceilings. Fresco painters need to work quickly and skilfully and the fresco can be applied using two different techniques. The 'true' fresco includes three coats of plaster, sand and marble dust and after the first two coats the artist applies an outline of his design. The artists then paints over the third layer tracing the outline underneath and the fresco becomes an integral part of the surface. The 'dry' fresco is made by soaking dry walls with lime water and then painting while wet. The pigments do not penetrate the plaster as in 'true' fresco.

Oil on Panel - Leonardo da Vinci

Most large paintings in Europe that were not frescoes, were created on panel. Painting on wood until the emergence of canvas was the norm and poplar or oak the wood of choice. To prepare the wood for oil paints a layer of animal skin glue was applied and then ground chalk applied. Next the artist made outlines on the panel using fine brushes or diluted paint before applying oil paints in fluid, sleek layers.

Oil on Canvas - Claude Monet

Oils binding together dry colour pigments into a thick paste allowed paints to dry slowly so facilitating the artist to adjust their paintings over time. As a result of new paint technology canvas stretched over a wooden frame gradually replaced the more expensive wooden panels. Canvas provides a pliable working surface, is cheap, lightweight, portable and adds subtle texture to finished paintings. As with panel a surface preparation is needed. A glue barrier and preparatory coating all over the canvas to reinforce and smooth it is used.

Watercolour - John Constable

A versatile medium, watercolours have been used by artists for their transparency and ability to be applied in washes. Many of the pioneers of watercolour and landscape painting laid transparent washes one over the other. This helped leave the white of the paper as highlights. Successive layers enriched colours, which they lifted and modified as they worked, emphasising the techniques versatility.

Impasto - Vincent van Gogh

The Italian word impasto means paste and describes extremely thickly applied paint. A method not encouraged by European art academies. Often creating coarse textured surfaces, only heavy-bodied paints can be applied as impasto. Some artists used palette knives to achieve certain affects and with the availability of ready mixed paints, the paint could be squeezed directly onto the canvas. With certain textures being able to suggest fabrics or wrinkled skin, folds in clothing or glinting jewellery.

Silkscreen - Andy Warhol

Patented in 1907, the modern form of screen-printing used silk as a screen to create high quality printed fabrics and wallpapers. This was later improved upon with various chemicals and emulsions to create smoother results. The process today involves the screen – now often made of cotton or nylon – being stretched tightly over a wooden frame. Artists then place stencils on the screen and lay paper or fabric beneath whilst forcing thick ink through the mesh, which adheres to the shape of the stencils. Screen-printed images of Marilyn Monroe, Campbell soup cans and dollar bills became synonymous with the technique.

Select Architecture and Art (including location)

Lascaux Cave Paintings – Montignac, France

In 1940 a series of colourful paintings was discovered in southwestern France. The elaborate images were made during the Stone Age up to 20000 years ago. They include wild animals, strange symbols and some human figures. Some 2000 images have been painted with colours made from burnt wood, bones or river clay and mud. These images are so fragile that a person's breath can cause damage. These caves are therefore no longer open to the public.

Lion Man (Lowenmensch) – Museum of Ulm, Germany

The carving made from Ivory is more than 40000 years old and was found in a German cave in 1939. It is the oldest known example of art that depicts the figure of a living creature. The figure has both human and animal features. It was carved out of a mammoth tusk. Although only about 30 cm tall, it would have taken many hours to carve using simple stone tools. The Lion Man shows us that even in harsh prehistoric times it was still important for the living to create artistic or religious objects.

Great Pyramid and Sphinx of Giza – Egypt

The great pyramid was the world's tallest man-made structure for an incredible 3800 years. More than 140 metres tall it was built as a tomb for a powerful pharaoh, Khufu, who died in 2566BC. Nearby is a mysterious 73 metre long statue of a mythical creature called a

Sphinx. It has the body of a lion and the head of a human, no one knows who built it or why. The four main structures at Giza are (in descending height) the Great Pyramid (Khufu) the pyramid of Khafre, the pyramid of Menkaure and the Sphinx of Giza, which guards the entrance to the site.

Rosetta Stone – British Museum, London

This large black stone is more than 2200 years old. The writing on it is an official message from a council of priests praising the pharaoh Ptolemy V Epiphanes. Because the writing is in two different languages and three different scripts, the discovery of the stone in 1799, now made it possible to understand the ancient Egyptian writing called hieroglyphics. Before the Rosetta Stone was found the pictures used in this writing were like a secret code that no one could decipher. From this stone a hieroglyphic alphabet could then be formulated and used to read subsequently discovered Egyptian antiquities.

Tomb of Tutankhamun – Egypt

The gold treasures found in an Egyptian tomb in 1922 were so spectacular that they have made the young boy king Tutankhamun the most famous of all the ancient Egyptian pharaohs. Not much is known about him, but his grave is one of the richest ever found in Egypt. A mural painted on the north wall of the burial chamber depicts Tutankhamun's journey to the afterlife. According to ancient Egyptian religion this was a dangerous journey that took a long time. In the mural, Tutankhamun can be seen meeting the god Osiris (the god of fertility, agriculture, the afterlife, the dead, resurrection, life, and vegetation.) and the goddess Nut (the goddess of the sky, stars, cosmos, mothers, astronomy, and the universe) along his journey.

The most impressive treasure from his tomb is arguably the Tutankhamun mask. It is made of solid gold and the bright blue stone Lapis Lazuli. Several ornate model boats were also found, as Egyptians believed that they would be needed for transport into the afterlife. Egyptian hieroglyphics can be found all over Egyptian tombs listing the good deeds of the people buried there.

Machu Picchu – Peru

An abandoned city situated 2400 metres up in the Andes Mountains. It was built high on some cliffs for the Inca king Pachacuti. Incas were skilled builders with their buildings made to survive earthquakes. They carried all the stone for construction on foot or using Llamas. The Inca Empire was eventually destroyed by Spanish invaders who came looking for gold. Centuries later, despite the high remote location, the ruins are still well preserved and one of the most visited sites in South America.

Sistine Chapel – Vatican City

The Italian artist Michelangelo's fresco masterpiece can be seen on the ceiling of this highly decorated private chapel in the Pope's palace. The equally stunning wall paintings are by other famous European artists. It took Michelangelo four years just to paint the ceiling. At a time when most people were illiterate, his large and complex images told the biblical stories of Adam and Eve and how god created the earth.

Mona Lisa – Louvre Museum, France

The most famous painting in the world is surprisingly small – only 77 cm high and 55 cm wide. This single painting is estimated to be worth a billion pounds or more. No one can be certain of its exact value because it has not been bought or sold since the 1500s. The portrait by Leonardo originally belonged to a French king and later to French emperor Napoleon. People have tried to damage the painting at least three times by throwing objects at it or spraying it with paint. As we know it has been stolen once and took two years to get back. Today it is displayed behind thick, bulletproof glass. A law has been passed making it impossible for anyone to sell the painting.

Faberge Eggs – Russia, Switzerland, UK

Peter Carl Faberge was the greatest jeweller of the late 1800s and early 1900s. His most famous creations were a number of elaborate enamelled Easter eggs. He made them for Russian tsars Alexander III and Nicholas II. Each one contained a different surprise. One egg included a miniature gold clockwork train, while another revealed a tiny mechanical peacock and another was the Imperial Coronation Egg (1897) containing a glittering imperial coach. Only about 46 have survived and several now belong to King Charles III. A single one of these eggs can sell for millions of pounds.

In the James Bond film Octopussy (1983), the Coronation Egg forms an important part of the plot. 009 discovers a smuggling scheme and steals a fake version of the egg and is killed as he delivers it to the British Ambassador at his residence in West Berlin. This alerts MI6 and 007 to numerous priceless Imperial Russian treasures being supplied to exiled prince and avid art collector Kamal Khan. This is being facilitated by a rogue Kremlin general who, ultimately, is seeking to expand Soviet control into Western-Central Europe.

Cullinan Diamond – Tower of London, UK

The largest diamond ever discovered was found just 9 metres below the surface in South Africa in 1905. It weighed more than 600 grams and was presented to British King Edward VII. The king had it cut into more than 100 different gems. They now form part of the British Crown Jewels. The largest gems are in the Imperial State crown and a sceptre. It is impossible to say how much they are now worth considering their current placement. In 1905 the mine owner was paid £150,000 for the original diamond, more than £15 million today.

Stradivarius Stringed Instruments – Palacio Real Museum, Madrid

Musicians agree that the best violins ever produced were made in Italy by Antonio Stradivari, also called Stradivarius. From 1666 until his death in 1737 he made stringed instruments such violas, harps and cellos – but his violins are the most famous. Even after more than two centuries five hundred or so of his violins still exist. The highest price ever paid for one is £9.5 million and many of them are kept in museums or private collections. The Palacio Real Museum has the largest public collection, with a viola, a cello and two violins. Some Stradivarius instruments are still played today, lent by generous owners to the top musicians in the world. Although not considered artworks they have been included here because they are so unique and many are kept in museums.

In the James Bond film The Living Daylights (1987) 007 comes into contact with Kara Milovy a cellist/sniper, in Bratislava. We first see Milovy playing in an orchestra, then we see her as a sniper. Despite being ordered to kill the sniper 007 chooses to injure her instead, by shooting her firearm from her hand. Later in the film Milovy tells 007 the cello is a Stradivarius and called The Lady Rose. In a subsequent scene they use it to escape over the border into Austria, via snow covered terrain, seated in the cello case and using the endpin of the Stradivarius to steer the case.

Chapter 3
Antiquities

Antiquities are the material remains of the past left behind by the generations that came before our own. Also called artefacts, relics, cultural objects and cultural property antiquities can be extremely old. Over ninety-nine percent of all human antiquities are the only real source of information we have about the past and as we know, history only begins with the introduction of written records around 5000BC. So the antiquities of all cultures and periods, whether with or without written evidence, provide us with that information and it is often archaeology alone that unearths these objects. Most art crime, as much as seventy-five percent, involves antiquities which may have been looted directly from the ground. However, as we are considering and studying antiquities already looted, as well as previously undiscovered, it is hard to properly verify this figure.

Eight Famous Antiquities

Dead Sea Scrolls

Estimated to have been written somewhere between 300BC and 100AD these scrolls were made of papyrus, parchment and copper and discovered in caves in the Red Sea area in 1946. Written mainly in Hebrew, Arabic and Greek they are made up of numerous fragments and are the earliest manifestation of the Bible. Sections of the scrolls are currently on view at the Israel Museum, Jerusalem.

Standard of Ur

The Standard is a chest type construction with inscriptions and decorative mosaic work and is made from bitumen, limestone and lapis lazuli originating around 2600BC in Sumer. The original function of this antiquity cannot be confirmed and is thought to have been a storage vessel for a musical instrument or religious items, rather than a military standard. It is located in the British Museum, London.

The Jade Dragon from Hongshan (1st Dragon of China)

The earliest known Chinese depiction of a dragon is a stylised C-shaped representation made in jade (green in colour). It belonged to the Hongshan Culture (prior to the dynasties mentioned earlier) which existed between 4500 and 3000BC in the Yellow River valley region. It is located in the National Museum of China, Beijing.

Mask of Tutankhamun

A classic antiquity made mainly from gold and lapis lazuli. It dates from around 1323BC and was discovered by Howard Carter in 1925. Found in a tomb in the Valley of the Kings it is now housed in the Egyptian Museum, Cairo. Howard Carter was a famous British archaeologist and Egyptologist. He had an early interest in Egyptian antiquities due to access, in his younger years, to a sizeable collection of Egyptian antiquities in the now demolished Didlington Hall Norfolk, England. He later began working in Egypt under the tutelage of experienced diggers. In 1899 Carter was appointed Inspector of Monuments for Upper Egypt in the Egyptian Antiquities Service. Based in Luxor he oversaw a number of excavations on behalf of the Egyptian government. In 1907 he began work for Lord Carnarvon who was the chief financial backer on many of the Carter Egyptian excavations, culminating in the discovery of the tomb.

Mask of Agamemnon

A gold funeral mask from ancient Greece dated 1550-1500BC recovered from an archaeological site seventy five miles south-west of Athens. The mask has been described as the Mona Lisa of antiquity and is displayed in the National Archaeological Museum of Athens.

Francois Vase

The Francois Vase is decorated in black and bronze and was used for wine. Described as a milestone antiquity in the development of ancient Greek pottery. Dated to 570-560 BC, it is now in the Museum of Archaeology in Florence.

The Orator

The Orator is a bronze sculpture of Aulus Metellus, a senator in the Roman Republic. Dated 110-90BC and recovered in Tuscany it is now in the Museum of Archaeology in Florence.

Laocoon and His Sons

The figures are life-size and over 2 metres in height showing the priest and his two sons being attacked by sea serpents. Dated 27BC - 68AD it has been one of the most famous ancient Greek sculptures ever since it was excavated in Rome in 1506 and placed on public display in the Vatican Museum where it remains.

Archaeology

Archaeology is a science which studies past human cultures through the examination of human remains, antiquities and environmental data and has connections to the fields of history and anthropology. It first started as a western engagement but has since become a vital practice across the world. Archaeology comes from the Greek word arkhaiologia, meaning a discourse about ancient things. One essential task of the archaeologist is to locate and record the whereabouts of archaeological sites. To do this the main types of investigation are ground and ariel surveys, undertaken using all available technology. Any first assessment is always of the site - Size, Type and Layout.

Three tactics that can then be used for the ground survey of a potential archaeological site and we see these quite often in the media. A ground survey is where a study of the distribution of surviving visual features (i.e. buildings) is conducted as well as collecting and recording any smaller fragments (antiquities) scattered across the land. Sub-surface detection is mainly carried out in a traditional manner by using different types of long metal probing rods. Some strike solids or hollows, others are used to bring up samples of soil from the bottom. Ground-remote sensing is also used as probing can sometimes overly disturb the soil. Sensing devices can either be active passing energy through the soil such as radar penetrating and then analyse the response. Or passive using magnetism such as metal detection devices scanned across the ground.

For an ariel survey planes and more recently drones can be used. These provide scanning of a larger site area and again often seen in the media. With the technology available, archaeologists are now able to survey areas which are hard to access by land as well as radar deployment which is also ground penetrating. This then allows for larger scale mapping of any site and can save the archaeologist time, with better indication of where best to excavate the site first.

After surveys are completed excavation retains a central role, as it yields the most reliable evidence needed by archaeologists. For different types of sites different methods will be used and two of the most common are again ones we see in the media. Trenches and test pits are used to evaluate the stratigraphy (rock, soil and geographical timescales) of a site before a decision is made on whether or not to start a site excavation. Important so as to not waste time, money and resources at the very outset. From this a smaller area of excavation, the most common form of excavation, can then take place. This is because the extent of the features to be uncovered have now determined the size of the area of excavation. This area can then move and extend as the excavation proceeds.

Context

Stratigraphy is concerned with geology. It is extremely important in the excavation of antiquities and just as important, the theft of them from the actual ground in which they have potentially been covered up for thousands of years. To simplify it, for the purpose of introductory information, stratigraphy provides a geological explanation of how layers of strata (rock and soil) are laid down on top of each other over time. Each element of these layers is what is known as a context. The task of the archaeologist is to identify each context and to trace the boundaries between these contexts. This may be detectable by changes in soil colour, texture or composition. If the context of an antiquity is not known or discoverable it is, for obvious reasons, of little use to archaeologists. So in a perfect world all antiquities would be discovered by them, alone.

Looting

Context, as we now know, is the crucial raw foundation through which archaeologists reconstruct the past. When an antiquity is stolen from the ground that key to the mystery of the ancient, that precious context, is destroyed. And it can never ever be recovered. Without context we have no starting point with which to construct the history of an object because looted antiquities introduce false information. Often looters will destroy or toss aside historically important objects in search of easily sold objects made of gold or precious metals.

There are three links in this chain of theft. Antiquities looting, antiquities smuggling and antiquities sales. When a looted antiquity appears on the market without context, we can only guess where it came from and what it was used for and its relation to human history. These guesses are almost certainly incorrect most of the time. In 1993 archaeologist Colin Renfrew asserted in the pages of the Archaeology Magazine that collectors are in fact the real looters. This is because the supply side of the antiquities chain demonstrates a classic imbalance between rich and poor. Individuals who engage in the illicit excavation of archaeological sites for saleable cultural antiquities, in the main, do so due to extreme poverty. It has been argued that they have very few economic opportunities and they are looting for survival, not profit. Looting has happened all around the world, with prominence particularly in Peru, Egypt and Greece.

With hundreds of thousands of archaeological sites in the world it is not possible to protect them all because many archaeological sites that are rich in antiquities, are in poorer parts of the developing world. The authorities in those countries often feel they have bigger problems to deal with than heritage protection. Additionally nations of origin, such as those in the Middle East and South America, are justifiably reluctant to sell or lose to foreign museums many objects that are unearthed legitimately by archaeologists. As a consequence this further fuels the illicit trade in antiquities by increasing demand, which can only be met by illegal activity.

Many archaeological sites are still in remote locations with no infrastructure, communities or basic utilities. These remote locations can be hotbeds for all sorts of activity relating to the looting, smuggling and sale of antiquities and there are a lot of archaeological sites that more than any one country could hope to protect on the ground. Peru, for example, has over 200,000 monuments and archaeological sites from its 4000 years of history and many of these are located in remote desert or jungle regions. This clearly tells us that security solutions to the antiquities smuggling problem should not only be focused on its source and solely on the looters. Efforts by governments, law enforcement, dealers and museum purchasers should be made on breaking up smuggling routes and on seriously discouraging the buyers at auctions.

The Antiquities Market

The two largest market centres for the sale of antiquities are New York and London. Antiquities which are looted from source countries are routinely smuggled to these cities to be sold by global art dealers and auction houses to other dealers, private collectors and museums. Provenance details in the form of documented history of an antiquity, regarding previous ownership and sale do not always accompany the antiquity or made readily available. Therefore, in many cases it is impossible for buyers to tell whether the antiquity they buy has been recently looted or not. Clearly for the buyer and international antiquities markets, reputationally, that is not good.

However, with recent changes in attitudes and the appreciation of potentially 'never to be recovered' antiquities, there has been a cultural shift change from governments most at risk from the practice. Subsequent laws have prevented the removal of looted antiquities from countries such as Egypt and Peru. Regardless, dealers have found a way to continue to smuggle antiquities across borders bound for the main market centres. Other dealers and museum buyers are well aware of this, but international market sentiment and practice have failed to match the legal efforts of effected states. Such are the prizes on offer. The fact of the matter is that this activity is that of the white-collar criminal.

It can be argued that for both dealers and museum buyers there is an ongoing desire to satisfy their conscience towards the purchase of what are suspected looted antiquities. By a combination of ignoring what others in the art world might think of them and by constructing their own personal interpretation and justification for buying an antiquity, when people eventually start asking questions. To test this theory in 2001 academic research was undertaken, a total of forty interviews were conducted in Melbourne, Sydney, New York, London, Geneva, Bangkok and Hong Kong with the focus on southeast Asian antiquities. Many of those interviewed fell into the category of key informants and included some of the world's most important and successful dealers.

From interview data dealers, collectors and museum buyers not surprisingly reject any accusations that they are the catalysts for looting. They deny that the culture and heritage of a country are damaged by their actions. Whilst simultaneously devaluing the worth of archaeological endeavour. There are two key points that repeated themselves here. First, they dispute that the looting of sites is harmful as they argue that many digs discover duplicate items that do not provide for new archaeological knowledge. Second, they continually appeal to the moral high ground of antiquity preservation and access to view them, such as in museums. Seemingly over and above the work of archaeologists, the rights of the source countries and indeed international law.

Indiana Jones and Antiquities – Fiction vs Fact

Dr Henry Jones Jr was an American professor of archaeology most famously known as Indiana Jones. Prior to World War II Jones secured a teaching position at Marshall College in Bedford Connecticut and worked under the head of the department Dr Marcus Brody. Himself an archaeologist, historian and lecturer. Brody was previously a curator for several prominent museums in New York and Washington DC (where the main museums of antiquity in the United States are factually located today). Marshall College had its own museum which was a subsidiary branch of the National Museum. Brody also served as its curator and paid for many of the minor antiquities that Jones retrieved on his expeditions.

Throughout his career Jones sought out and located numerous famous mythological antiquities, here I have chosen to omit antiquities from the Temple of Doom film. The most prominent antiquities were the Fertility Idol, the Ark of the Covenant – which once recovered, was famously stored in a wooden crate amongst thousands of others in Hanger 51 in the Nevada Desert. As a young Indiana in the Last Crusade film the Cross of Coronado, the Holy Grail and with the enemy now the Russians the Crystal Skull of Akator. All of which placed him in conflict with different antagonists across the globe.

His primary antagonists were Rene Belloq, initially assisted by Gestapo officer Arnold Ernst Toht in Raiders of the Lost Ark (1981) and Walter Donovan, assisted by Elsa Schneider, in the Last Crusade (1989). Both of these were working under the direction of the Adolf Hitler and the Nazi regime who had a vivid interest in the occult and archaeological antiquities. This prompted Nazi research and recovery expeditions into specific biblical antiquities, ultimately to be used as weapons against Nazi enemies. This is highlighted in the Raiders film when Jones and Brody are visited by US Army

Intelligence officers. Jones opens a large antique bible and shows them a colour illustration depicting the power of the Ark, it is this illustration that makes the military men realize why Hitler is extremely interested in acquiring it.

Rene Belloq was a French archaeologist and a career at the Louvre, as a curator, ended when Belloq was suspected of organising and funding a looting expedition in Iran. Afterwards he became a mercenary archaeologist to whomever could afford him, with the use of increasingly unethical methods to acquire valuable antiquities. The activities of Belloq were initially assisted in Raiders by Gestapo officer Arnold Ernst Toht. The Third Reich Special Antiquities Collection was a branch of the government of Nazi Germany that collected occult and biblical antiquities and send Toht to collaborate with Belloq. He was a skilled torturer and interrogator and a firm believer in the Third Reich and its principles.

Walter Donovan was a wealthy American industrialist and collector of antiquities living in Manhattan. He had already donated several antiquities to the National Museum when his copper miners discover a stone tablet in Turkey. Engraving on the tablet told of the existence of the Holy Grail. Obsessed with the immortality which would come with the Grail Donovan partnered with the Nazis, unbeknown to Jones. The activities of Donovan and the Nazis were assisted by Elsa Schneider. She was an Austrian art professor and former Olympic swimmer who also desired the Grail and like Donovan, keeps her involvement with the Nazis secret.

Fertility Idol (Peru)

Chachapoyas is a province of the Amazonian region of northern Peru. The Chachapoyan civilization was real and conquered by the Incas until the Spanish conquistadors arrived, the culture was a genuine subject of interest for scientists under the Nazis. The

Raiders film attributes the Chachapoyans as having built the fictitious Temple of the Warriors from which Jones escapes and is ultimately forced to hand over the Idol to Belloq. Jones had previously been alerted of the danger to the Idol when a score of golden, purportedly Chachapoyan, figurines began to appear on the antiquities market. Jones and Brody believed that the hitherto undiscovered Chachapoyan temples had been located and were now being looted. A six inch high golden antiquity it depicts the Chachapoyan goddess of fertility and for the purposes of the film, the prop is based on the Dumbarton Oaks Birthing Figure. This is a figurine of a woman giving childbirth in the squatting position. It is part of the Dumbarton Oaks Estate collection in Washington DC. The figure is possibly carved from greenstone. Its real age is of ongoing academic debate some suggesting it is not of antiquity, but more modern, whilst others question the figures stylistic features.

Ark of the Covenant (Egypt)

The classic Indiana Jones relic with a huge biblical significance. The Ark is described as a pure gold covered chest with an elaborate lid adorned with two winged cherubs. In the second book of the bible, the Book of Exodus, it narrates the story of the exodus in which the Israelites leave slavery in Egypt, who God has chosen as his people. It was said to contain the two stone tablets of the Ten Commandments, Aaron's Rod and a pot of manna. The Ark was built by Moses and his followers under instructions from God over a forty day period. The Ark was then carried for forty years by the Israelites as they sought land for their new nation. In Raiders Brody remarks that whoever carries the Ark before it is deemed invincible. Stories in the bible relate to the River Jordan drying out as the Ark is carried across it and how the Ark causes the city walls of Jericho to fall.

However, a few years later the elders of Israel decided to take the Ark out onto the battlefield to assist them against the Philistines but they were heavily defeated and the Ark captured. It is said this happened because the Ark had not been consulted by the elders before battle commenced. The Philistines took the Ark to several places in their country and at each place various misfortune mysteriously befell them. The Ark was quickly returned to the Israelites, and eventually removed to what is modern day Abu Ghosh six miles west of Jerusalem. The Ark was eventually sent to the newly built Solomon's Temple, the first temple to be built in Jerusalem, and housed in a special inner room. In 587BC, the Babylonians (originating from Iraq/Syria) destroyed Jerusalem and the temple. There is no further record of what became of the Ark in the bible. The final location of the Ark is disputed by both religious leaders and academics, but its existence is not. Jewish history states it was carried off to Babylon and never returned, whilst another theory is that it returned to Abu Ghosh, another that it is buried somewhere on the Temple Mount in Jerusalem.

In Raiders, Jones has to acquire the fictitious Headpiece to the Staff of Ra a much sought-after bronze medallion, which was originally designed as a means to reveal the location of the Ark. Around the headpiece back and front, written in Hebrew, were instructions on how long the staff (a simple shaft of wood) should be made on which the headpiece would sit. The film suggests that the final secret resting place of the Ark is Egypt. The headpiece is placed atop the staff and used in the Map Room, located inside a chapel in the lost city of Tanis, to reveal the location of the Well of the Souls. This was the name of a vault inside a temple, the actual location of the hidden Ark

Later in the film the Ark is opened by Belloq and the Nazis on the small fictitious island Geheimhaven, meaning secret haven. It was a secret Nazi supply base located north of Crete possessing a submarine pen. The Ark is brought to the island to examine its contents before taking it to Berlin and presenting it to Hitler. On the instructions of Belloq the Ark is taken to the highest point of the island, so a Jewish ritual can be conducted whilst opening the Ark.

For the ritual Belloq dresses as a High Priest of Israel, an ancient chief religious official, in full ceremonial attire. In the Book of Exodus instructions were given by God as to how the priest should look and included, over a robe, a garment called an Ephod. Made of linen with gold, blue, purple and scarlet in two front and back parts, it is secured at the shoulders by two onyx stones set in gold. The front and back of the Ephod were made to be as one garment by a sash. Then a breastplate is worn over this which is a pouch about 22 cm square, made of beautifully woven material. On the front of the breastplate are fastened twelve precious stones in four rows of three and a priestly turban is also worn. On opening the Ark there appears to be only the sand remains of the Ten Commandments before spirits begin to rise up from the relic.

Cross of Coronado (Utah)

The Last Crusade starts in Utah in 1912, with a young Indiana Jones as a boy scout in a failed attempt to retrieve the Coronado from treasure hunters in a cave system. The fictitious Cross is a jewel-encrusted golden crucifix with a chain and named after the real Spanish conquistador Francisco Vasquez de Coronado. It is believed to contain an actual piece of the cross upon which Jesus was crucified. It was given to Francisco by another conquistador but he eventually lost it. At some point the cross was boxed and hidden away in a burial site within the cave complex, in what would become the US state of Utah and then fell into legend.

The Cross is based on the Cross of Justin II, also known as the Vatican Cross. Justin II ruled the Byzantine Empire during 500AD and it is kept in the Treasury building in the Vatican City. It is claimed to be the oldest surviving reliquary of the True Cross. It is a jewelled cross with silver gilt and adorned with jewels in gold settings and looks very much like the Cross of Coronado. The cross bears a Latin inscription reading 'For the wood of the cross with which human Christ was overcome by the enemy.'

Holy Grail (Turkey)

The Holy Grail was believed to be the cup that Jesus drank from during the Last Supper. It was also used to catch his blood at his crucifixion after being stabbed by the Spear of Destiny. It was said that the Grail could give to whomever drank from it eternal life and had the power to heal any injuries, diseases or infections. In the Last Crusade the fictitious Grail Temple in the Canyon of the Crescent Moon, Hatay (modern-day Turkey) was the location for the Holy Grail. In the year 1000AD a secret society built the temple in a hidden gorge and the rock carved facade used in the film is actually the Al-Khazneh temple in Petra, Jordan. This group became the Brotherhood of the Cruciform Sword sworn to keep it safe from discovery and misuse, by any means necessary.

The stone tablet found in the copper mine owned by Donovan is broken and missing vital information that Jones needs to track down. Below the Venice library Jones discovers the tomb of a knight of the First Crusade Sir Richard (not to be confused with King Richard The Lionheart) and in the tomb his shield has been placed on his body. Jones and Elsa Schneider then arrive to retrieve a rubbing of the inscription engraved on this shield, completing the required missing stone tablet information. Later in the temple Donovan assumes the Grail to be a fabulous golden chalice encrusted with jewels and inlaid with silver. The real Grail was a simple, worn clay cup of a carpenter.

The history of any real Holy Grail is much more complicated and as in biblical situations, many religious groups and countries make claim to the existence of a Grail. In various and extensive literature on the matter since the 1200s the Holy Grail seems to have been designated as the cup used to catch the blood of Jesus after crucifixion and another cup the Holy Chalice, in subsequent literature, is designated as the cup used at the last supper. Thereafter, the Holy Grail became interwoven with the legend of the Holy Chalice. A cup kept in the Spanish Cathedral of Valencia has been purported since medieval times to be the Holy Chalice. The cup is made of dark red agate and mounted on a stem with two curved handles. It is preserved in a chapel consecrated to it where it still attracts the faithful on pilgrimage. The antiquity, in relation to Indiana Jones, has never been accredited with any supernatural powers.

Crystal Skull of Akator (Brazil)

In the 2008 film the Kingdom of the Crystal Skull, the Crystal Skull of Akator was part of the remains of one of the thirteen interdimensional beings that had visited the Amazonian region some seven thousand years before. They had helped the ancient civilisation that existed there build a city, that the conquistadors called El Dorado, known in the film as Akator. The beings stood some nine feet tall and their heads were elongated. Instead of bone, their skeletons were made of a crystalline property which held magnetic qualities. The thirteen thought and acted as a hive mind and a single being. For some unexplained reason in the film, the beings remained there dormant in an inner temple, as crystal skeletons.

Centuries later the conquistador Francisco de Orellano found the inner temple after discovering El Dorado. Along with gold treasure he took the crystal skull of one such skeleton. On their return to Peru, Orellana and his men were killed by Nazca Chauchilla Cemetery warriors who were dressed like skeletons. Orellano thought he was being attacked by the living dead. The warriors then buried Orellano and his men in a secret grave chamber in the cemetery, with their bodies being completely mummified and Orellana buried along with a gold death mask and the crystal skull. The skull had a very elongated back of the head and was incredibly magnetic, even attracting metals such as gold that were not magnetic by nature. Legend said that whoever would eventually return the skull, would receive great power.

In the interesting background to the film, the real facts about Akator and the crystal skull seem more like fiction. The film creatively blended three real life mythical elements of El Dorado (known in the film as the City of Gold) with the lost underground city of Akakor hoax (renamed in the film as Akator) as well as the films back story about crystal skulls (specifically mentioning the Mitchell-Hedges skull) which is discussed during the diner scene.

El Dorado was a mythical empire located in Colombia, said to be rich in gold and precious jewels. The myth grew amongst the conquistadors when rumour spread that their ruler engaged in a ceremony whereby the body was completely covered in gold dust. During the time of the conquistadors, fascinated by the New World and believing that a hidden city of immense wealth existed, numerous expeditions were mounted to search for this treasure, all of which ended in failure. Akakor is the name of an alleged ancient underground city located somewhere between Brazil, Bolivia and Peru which was subsequently revealed as the product of a hoax. It was a city described by journalist Karl Brugger, based on interviews with a self-proclaimed Brazilian Indian chief Tatunca Nara, in his book The Chronicle of Akakor (1976). Nara was later exposed as being Gunther Hauck a German-Brazilian jungle guide. So for the film, elements of the story from The Chronicle of Akakor were used and conflated with El Dorado, with the name being changed to Akator.

Crystal skulls are made of white quartz and often claimed to be of South American antiquity. However, these claims have been refuted because all of the specimens made available for scientific studies demonstrated they were manufactured during the 1800s in Europe, at the height of interest in ancient culture. Despite claims presented in popularizing literature, legends of crystal skulls with mystical powers do not figure in genuine South American mythology or archaeology. With none of the skulls in museum collections showing any provenance from documented excavations conducted in the region. Although museums had acquired skulls earlier, it was Eugene Boban a French antiquities dealer, who is most associated with museum collections of crystal skulls.

Perhaps the most famous and enigmatic skull was allegedly discovered in 1924 by the daughter of adventurer and author Frederick Mitchell-Hedges. The skull is made from a block of clear quartz and the lower jaw is detached. It was claimed to be found buried under a collapsed altar inside a temple in what is now Belize. Mitchell-Hedges asserted it as being at least 3600 years old and was used by the High Priest of an ancient civilisation when performing ceremonies. In these rituals he willed death with the help of the skull, death invariably followed. Recent evidence has come to light showing that Mitchell-Hedges had purchased the skull in 1943 from art dealer Sydney Burney. The skull was scientifically examined in 2007 at the Smithsonian in Washington DC, leading to the conclusion that the skull was probably carved in the 1930s. The conclusion was that the design of this skull was most likely based on a skull on display in the British Museum, which has been exhibited continuously since 1898.

Chapter 4
Theft of Art

Having looked at antiquities and the act of looting from sites this chapter will concentrate on the theft of art, which in the main, tends to be paintings. Historically a financial sum cannot be put on art theft. Much art crime goes unreported or undiscovered and its value is fluid. A painting worth £1 million can two years later be valued at £5 million reliant on authenticity, rarity, the interest of collectors, current art world economics or newly discovered information regarding the artist. Regardless, this crime affects the art world with subsequent illegal profits allegedly running into the billions as suggested by the FBI and Interpol. Who also indicate that this type of crime is significant enough to be ranked as the third largest criminal trade in recent times.

Despite significant law enforcement activity in this area by the FBI, Interpol and the Italian and French police, they do not generally provide adequate public data. Despite this, academics using law enforcement data that is publicly available as well as other open source material have cleverly tried to come up with a list of who is actually stealing all the art. A list of seven types of thief has been suggested with some crossover and the largest part of the debate concerns the actual amount of involvement by organised crime. Additionally, figures from the Art Loss Register concerning worldwide theft indicated the following premises from which art is actually stolen (ranked in descending order) were private residences, corporate offices, commercial art galleries, museums, churches, art that was in transit and warehouses.

Mr Big

The individual who is a private collector who commissions the theft. The idea of a super-rich collector has been used since the time of the James Bond movies. When the very famous painting is stolen, the narrative is that the theft must have been to order and makes sense. This is because crucially, the thief does not have the necessary art expertise nor the necessary illegal art market contacts to move on a very famous painting. This theory usually prevails when specific art is stolen from a specific museum and never seen again - suggesting that it may now be hanging in the luxurious office of Mr Big for their own pleasure.

Compulsive Thief

A common thief meets collector individual who can steal a lot, but not necessarily the famous art. They too seem to keep the art for their own enjoyment but have been known to return art anonymously once they are aware that law enforcement may be closing in on them. A compulsive thief generally wishes to avoid any prison time whatsoever, after all, their ad-hoc desires to possess artwork is not strong enough to accept the loss of their liberty for any period of time.

Organised Crime

This category fits in with the explanation that law enforcement often give for major art theft, with the aforementioned theft from the Isabella Stewart Gardner Museum in 1990 a prime example. Without doubt this had all the hallmarks of organised crime due to the size of the haul. Generally, it is suggested that since the 1960s most art crime has been perpetrated by, or on behalf of, international organised criminals. There are three suggested avenues for organised criminals to gain a famous work of art which cannot be sold on the open market. They are ransom, illegal market sale and more commonly, their use as collateral. As with the compulsive thief the organised criminal, involved in the theft of famous artwork, will be concerned with the risk of extensive prison time if arrested. Which always causes problems within a crime family, depending on who gets convicted. However, the number of known art crimes does not necessarily justify that this organised crime link can explain the majority of all art thefts, post 1980.

Ideological Thief

A higher purpose for an art theft is not strange when you consider the motive. The thief can put a museum or government under pressure to give into their demands, especially if the artwork is of national and culture heritage significance. Effectively an irreplaceable piece. In 1961, Goya's the Duke of Wellington was stolen from the National Gallery in London. The thief demanded that £150,000 (£3.5 million today) be paid to a charity that would provide free of charge, radio and TV licences to the poor and elderly. When the demands were not met the painting was left at a railway station. Despite subsequent speculation surrounding the thief, it had transpired to be an overweight old man who had simply entered the building via a ladder that had been left there by construction workers. In popular culture the painting was seen hanging in the secret hideout of Dr No in the 1962 James Bond film, supposedly stolen to order, which at this point was still missing in the real world. There is also now a 2021 film, The Duke, staring Jim Broadbent and Helen Mirren which tells the story of the theft and the main protagonist.

Ransom

In most known cases museums, private collectors and certainly governments do not give in to ransom demands. Many paintings are surprisingly not insured, so a deal with an insurance company is impossible. Museums also refrain from paying ransom as generally they could not afford it, unless of course, they were to sell other artwork to raise the ransom but in many countries it is illegal to negotiate or pay a ransom. In a number of cases law enforcement officers have posed as potential buyers and met with the thieves at various locations, where they have offered the artwork. In other cases it is still unclear whether a ransom has been demanded and paid. This may be because the thief has realised the famous artwork cannot be sold safely or there are simply no buyers for it in the criminal world. Stolen paintings have also been left anonymously in random places. In reality it seems that a private, clandestine, arrangement may have been organised between the thief and the insurance company, museum, or collector.

Internal Thief

Data and research into theft from museums has found that eighty-three percent of thefts could be classed as internal. This meant that museum staff with privileged access to collections such as curators, conservationist, academics, security and gallery attendants had been involved. What is also a problem in relation to this category of theft is that museums hold vast collections, most of which are held in secure basement reserve stores. Again, these areas are to which the thief will have access regardless of their own concerns, as to whether for example, it is covered by door access control or CCTV which would implicate them. Internal theft is often repeated after an initial success and can go unnoticed for years.

Common Thief

These thefts in the main are concerned with paintings. A straightforward theft of artwork followed by an immediate sale. These thieves can work alone but usually in a team with other criminals who come up with an idea for a simple theft or are asked by other low-level criminals to steal and sell on specifically to them. The thefts, like most other common thefts, involve little planning and those committing the thefts are far from criminal masterminds. They are used because they are expendable and generally do not ask for much money and unlike the compulsive thief come collector, they are not bothered about prison time.

In conclusion it can be argued that the involvement of organised crime and Mr Big characters in art theft, is overplayed. Organised crime is suggested regularly by law enforcement but then only seems to involve very high profile and famous art theft, which does not happen very often. Likewise, the Mr Big concept seems to endure due to its representation in popular culture and mystery of the all-encompassing super criminal. It seems that ransom, the internal thief and the common thief, collectively, seem to dominate whatever data is publicly available.

Chapter 5
Provenance Research

Researching the origins of Art and Antiquities

In the art and antiquities world the origin and timeline of a piece of art is crucial. Mainly for its authenticity, valuation and ownership. The word provenance derives from the French word provenir meaning to originate. An ideal provenance provides a documentary record of owners' names, dates of ownership, methods of transference (such as inheritance) or sale through a dealer or auction and locations where the art was kept from the time of its creation by the artist until the present day. However, such complete and unbroken records of ownership are rare and most art contains gaps in provenance. Indeed it is more common for an object to have an incomplete ownership history than a complete one. While provenance research generally begins with art history resources, it often leads to other historical or genealogical information, which is particular evident in World War II era provenance research.

Provenance research can be difficult and time-consuming and the researcher needs the ability to think outside the box. Pieces of artwork are bought, sold and handed down constantly and thus provenance can grow at an extensive rate. Records that do exist may not be accurate so will require other evidence to corroborate their validity. Some archives have suffered damage or destruction due to wars or natural disasters. Private collectors may not have saved purchase records or created a record of transfer for sales. So once that sale is completed, it may be difficult or impossible to track its subsequent owners or to identify it as formerly belonging to a particular collector or collection. Tracing an objects ownership can be further complicated by the means with which a transfer takes place. The art may have been commissioned or purchased directly from the artist or at its first exhibition. Or it may, in the distant past, have been traded by the artist for art supplies or some other unrelated art goods.

Complicating the situation even further is the fact that forgers are notorious for creating false provenance documents thereby intentionally confusing the historical record. This means that each part of a provenance must be evaluated on its own merits and as already stated, corroborated if possible, with secondary evidence. If no corroboration is possible in the timeline, the researcher must note this. Subsequent researchers will then know this and that secondary information, therefore, will have a better chance of being corroborated in the future.

With provenance important for authenticity, valuation and ownership these three areas must always be considered during research, so time is not wasted on a possible multitude of documents that may be available. Provenance can bolster claims of a works authenticity. Inventory records of an object's presence in a particular collection or in an artist's studio provide strong evidence of that authenticity. As a consequence of establishing authenticity, a complete or almost trusted ownership history may have a positive impact on the value of a work of art. For ownership, transaction records and other proofs of sale or transfer help determine legitimacy, as well as provide a defence in repatriation or restitution claims. In some cases the presence of a red-flagged name in the provenance may indicate the artwork was stolen, subjected to a forced sale or otherwise misappropriated during the time of the Third Reich. Thus warranting important and crucial further research. This element of provenance is further discussed later in the Office of Strategic Services file 1945 chapter.

In conducting provenance research on a specific antiquity or piece of art, the researcher first gathers whatever information is available from the object itself. Without first hand access to examine an object itself, first rate provenance research would be very difficult to achieve. Photographs alone would not necessarily be able to confirm any alterations or conservation work on the art. The object is the most important primary resource in any research. The entire object must be examined for any inscriptions, dates or other distinctive marks. Other information can be gained from exhibition stickers and dealer/collectors marks. As well as transport and customs stamps, many of which can be found, surprisingly, on the rear of paintings.

Second, assess general art history records, whether in a library or using internet open source materials. This should stem from the information collected from the artwork itself. The researcher would start by checking the published works of the artist themselves, which often includes some provenance information, exhibition history, publication references and current owners. This can then be supplemented by all published sale references and exhibition catalogues. Exhibition catalogues are very useful in provenance research because there are numerous exhibitions in various museums and galleries across the globe, therefore providing valuable information for later use. They will provide a photograph and document the owner and location of an object at a specific time and some catalogues also list lenders. Although if the lender is a private collector it may not reveal the name of the owner at this point, in the artworks history.

Third, assess information concerning collectors and dealers and when a dealer or collector actually acquired an artwork. From here it is important to identify ancestors who may have inherited the work. Some museums, for example, can have significant information on the collectors that they acquire artwork from, such as the Louvre and the Getty Museum. The only way to confirm for sure if an artwork passed through a legitimate dealer is for the researcher to ask a dealer to check their files. However, as you would imagine, not all dealers make their files accessible due to client confidentiality.

Fourth, assess auction records which are generally easy to track, as they are public auctions in the main and useful for tracing appearances of individual works of art. Again, due to client confidentiality, names of sellers and buyers may not be printed in any subsequent publication of the auction, but the auction house may be willing to forward a letter of enquiry. It should also be noted that as many people attend auctions, for whatever reason, there may be more than one publication available on the same auction. The researcher must therefore consult all those publications, as some may contain vital information that others do not.

Provenance Researcher Checklist

A physical check of the work, dimensions, signatures, dates, inscriptions, condition and any change in the name of the work. Obtain various angled photographs of the work to constantly compare with existing photographic documentation

Trace and obtain all art history and general documentation/open source material regarding the artwork and importantly the artist

Trace and obtain all collectors and dealers information whether directly from collector/dealer, publication or open source information

Trace and obtain same from auction houses

Source and examine exhibition catalogues from museums and art galleries in which the artwork has appeared

List any written correspondence as part of any research which may include museums, collectors, dealers, auction houses, letters of enquiry and letters to suspected or potential ancestors or heirs

The researcher will cross reference and attempt to corroborate all information obtained

Complete a provenance style record for the artwork which can be subject to change in the future, subject to proper confirmation of any further evidence

World War II Provenance Researcher Checklist

The Nazi regime was responsible for the confiscation, sale, looting and destruction of millions of works of art and antiquities from, public and private collections throughout Nazi-occupied Europe. The scale of their systematic looting was unprecedented. Most items were stolen or forcibly taken from the private collections of Jews and other holocaust victims. Some of the stolen works entered the private collections of Nazi officials, notably Hermann Goering. Others were intended for Hitler's planned Furhrer Museum in Linz and others sold or traded for cash or other art. This checklist will help the researcher focus on the provenance of this type of art theft, in addition to the previous standard provenance checklist.

Research the gap in known ownership for art during the period between 1933 when Hitler came to power, until the end of the war in 1945

The gap 1933 to 1938 involved the invasion and occupation of Austria

The gap 1938 to 1945 involved the invasion and occupation of Poland

The gap 1940 to 1945 involved the invasion and occupation of France

Extremely careful research and identification of red-flag names appearing within existing provenances

The Art Looting Investigation Unit (ALIU) in the Office of Strategic Services (OSS) in the United States created a list after the war. It includes the name of virtually every person interrogated, investigated or even mentioned during the units investigation into art looting. Most of the individuals on the list were middlemen associated with looting activities. Whilst not considered to be owners or possessors of large quantities of looted art, would nonetheless, be individuals who would require further research and extreme caution in any provenance. They were mostly art experts and dealers who knew not only about art, but provenance documentation, its importance in sales and had the knowledge of how it could be altered permanently. Vitally important to know when conducting research.

Chapter 6
Fakes, Forgeries and Science

Fakes and Forgeries

When discussing fakes and forgeries in the world of art and antiquities, there can be lots of confusion when art is being presented as being by one artist, when it is actually by another. Likewise, when an antiquity is presented as being from a properly excavated site, when in fact, it is nothing more than a carefully constructed replica. Some countries, such as Turkey, have made the copying of important art and antiquities of cultural heritage a criminal offence. However, in other nation states, misrepresenting the artist of a painting or cultural background of an antiquity is not. As long as it is not passed off as such for financial gain, whereby the offence of fraud is then committed.

As everyone knows, the terms art fake and art forgery are always used interchangeably and the painters of fake art often referred to as art forgers. This crossover of language has been happening since modern times. However, this has meant the use of the correct legal terms have not been applied in everyday discussion. Effectively, in a legal context, art and antiquities can only be faked and documents can only be forged. This is important when you consider that the documentary provenance of art and antiquity is crucial when being bought and sold. When a fake painting is sold using a forged provenance document claiming its historical authenticity, you have the combination of fake and forgery coming together to commit a crime. Something, I suggest, happens quite often but then goes unreported to law enforcement. In terms of the actual art or antiquity, a fake painting can give an incorrect impression of an artist's technique and choice of subjects, whilst the fake antiquity could have a damaging effect on culturally important historical research. And then of course, on discovery of the fraud rendering both items worthless.

Science

Scientific methods have been increasingly used to assist in determining if an artwork is fake. However, even with this scientific input there are three areas of caution here. First, the science cannot always be used as a sole indicator. Authentication should always, if possible, be used in conjunction with a combination of provenance research, scientific methods and visual examination by art experts. For example, Dr Martin Kemp of Oxford University, is a renowned expert in the paintings of Leonardo, so has been consulted on a number of occasions concerning his paintings. Second, there must also be an awareness that the artist tasked with creating the fake may be one step ahead of the scientist and third, but most importantly, scientific methods can prove a work of art or antiquity is a fake but they cannot prove it is authentic. The main scientific methods currently in use are Microscopy, Mass Spectrometry, X-Ray, CT Scan and Infrared Reflectography.

Microscopy

This is a method concerning the high level magnification of images. By looking at a small paint sample from a painting under extreme magnification, much can be discovered. If stereo magnification is used, this allows for 3D visuals. This can allow the examiner to get a detailed look at how paint has been layered on an artwork and, crucially, see whether paint has been added at a much later date -

such as the signature of a famous artist. The method is also used for observing craquelure. Effectively the fingerprints of older paintings, that are very common and appear over time. Craquelure is the French term for the fine cracks in paint or varnish. It is a fine pattern of dense cracking formed on the surface of the paint and can be a result of drying, aging, intentional patterning, or a combination of all three. Craquelure assessment would include its direction, shape, spacing, thickness and organisation. If the correct craquelure is missing or incorrect, the examiner knows they have a fake painting. For example, the small rectangular cracks on the Mona Lisa are the correct shape for Italian paintings from that period.

Mass Spectrometry

Mass spectrometry is a technique with its origins in physics and is concerned with the quantity of something, versus its electrical discharge under scientific conditions. In the main it is an analysis for the paint used in art, specifically the type of pigment in the paint. So as to identify exactly what pigments are in a particular painting. The results are then shown in a chart and the examiner can then compare the masses present in the pigment sample to comparable known pigments. For example, the examiner can determine whether lead is present in what is thought to be a very old painting. Lead was commonly used by painters in the past, but because of the risk of lead poisoning it is now virtually obsolete in modern art. So, no lead in an old painting raises immediate questions about authenticity. Likewise, mass spectrometry can also detect the presence of pigments that were not yet created when the artwork being tested was supposedly made. If mass spectrometry shows that a supposed Leonardo painting contains pigment that was not manufactured until 1980, the examiner knows they have a fake painting.

X-ray

X-ray technology can also be used to determine whether a possible fake is painted on a reused canvas. Clever artists engaged in producing fake art know that you cannot paint what is meant to be an old painting onto a new canvas. So the artist will tend to paint over less valuable, but still old, artwork to try and create a more authentic fake. The reuse of canvasses was not uncommon in the art world many years ago. This is because starving artists from all periods sought to save money by painting over their own or other paintings, meaning the older painting(s) will always be under the newer painting. For example, a disputed 17th century painting is X-rayed and what is obviously a 19th century painting is found underneath, the examiner has a fake painting. Additionally, through art history research if it was found that an artist only painted on new canvass, the presence of any previous painting below the surface would be another strong indicator that the art is fake.

CT scan

This technique has become a game changer when dealing primarily with fake antiquities. Already used extensively to examine Egyptian mummies, CT imaging is ideal for the assessment of the internal structure of antiquities, particularly the inner density of its materials. A scan can help provide an internal signature of an antiquity with the material able to be scanned including wood, stone, clay, bone, ivory and some metals. The artist creating the fake antiquity can use real materials from the period in question which are placed on the surface of an item, with more modern materials used internally, hidden to the naked eye. These internal differing densities can be detected on a CT scan, helping identify crucial anomalies in an antiquity.

Infrared Reflectography

ART CRIME AND SECURITY

Historically, artists do not always paint a whole work directly onto a canvas with no plan whatsoever. It is common practice for an artist to make at least some marks, known as underdrawings, before and during the painting process to help guide the form and structure of the painting. Some artists use pencils others use paint. Whilst some use only tiny marks and others sketch nearly complete versions of the final painting. In nearly all instances artists use the same painting preparation technique continuously, in their own distinct way. Through the use of infrared reflectography, art scientists can see below the surface of a painting and investigate the otherwise-invisible sketches below. This technique is based on the fact that unlike light in our visual range, infrared light can penetrate the layers of pigment until it reaches the underdrawings of a painting. The infrared light is then reflected back into a specially designed camera which then produces an image of what is underneath. If whatever is below the surface of a painting deviates significantly from the acknowledged preparation method of a particular artist, the examiner can conclude that the painting is very likely a fake.

Han van Meegeren

Henricus Antonius 'Han' van Meegeren was a famous Dutch artist and producer of fake art portraits who operated during World War II. Many of his activities and motives during the war are still debated. He has been described as a gifted technician who when he painted, had every virtue except originality. His talent for producing and selling fake paintings fooled the world and eventually led to his trial for treason in the aftermath of World War II. When it became known that he had sold a fake painting to Hermann Goering during the Nazi occupation of the Netherlands, he became something of a national hero. His particular talent was for the production of paintings by Johannes Vermeer, another Dutchman and one of the most famous painters in the world. In popular culture reference is made to Han van Meegeren in the 2019 film The Last Vermeer. It is based on the book The Man Who Made Vermeers by Jonathan Lopez. It tells the story of van Meegeren, played by Guy Pearce and how he swindled millions of dollars out of the Nazis assisted by Dutch resistance fighter Joseph Piller. It was described as a fight against the Nazis and for the good of the Dutch people, or so he claimed, because his forgeries netted him an estimated $30 million.

Jan Vermeer was born in 1632 in the busy Dutch port city of Delft, which at the time had an extremely important role in world trade. So back then, where there was money, there was art. Delft became a centre for Dutch painters of the period who became known as the Old Masters, who painted during the Dutch Golden Age art movement, referred to in the art timeline chapter. Art experts suggest there were only thirty four works ever painted by Vermeer, making them extremely rare. This is exacerbated by the lack of records concerning his life, training and works but presents all sorts of possibilities to a producer of fake paintings. The works of Vermeer use the same structure, rooms, models and clothing. He also had a meticulous style, using extremely fine paints to produce almost photographic quality paintings, that particularly emphasised light and focus. He painted mostly interior scenes with normal people going about their everyday activities. His most famous paintings include Girl with the Pearl Earring, The Milkmaid, The Astronomer and The Concert.

Although not from Delft, van Meegeren loved the Old Masters of the Dutch Golden Age. While a perfectly adept painter critics viewed his art as displaying excellent technical talent but lacking in artistic originality. It has been suggested that it was this criticism that ultimately drove van Meegeren to get back at those critics by fooling them with fake Vermeers. The normal painter of fake art would attempt to avoid scientific and expert analysis however, van Meegeren wanted to actively deceive these very people. He realised that the presence of a previously undiscovered Vermeer would draw significant attention from all corners of the art world. He was extremely successful in his endeavours, for a while.

To facilitate his ongoing fake productions, van Meegeren had seemingly worked hard to create processes and practices that would help speed up that production. Processes which would cross reference with those mentioned above relating to science. However, with scientific advances, they would not have been successful today. He used Bakelite, a synthetic resin, to mix his paints instead of the more traditional oil. Oil paintings take a number of years to fully dry and his use of Bakelite allowed the fresh oil paint, when cooked in an oven, to harden and dry so that the painting would appear old if ever tested. He then perfected that skill of drying the painting in an oven to create the appropriate type and amount of cracking of the paint, the craquelure. He carefully selected the actual paints he used and whether it would be on canvas or wood panel and most importantly the type of brush used to paint the work. This was because Vermeer used specific brushes of badger hide that he had made himself. Eventually van Meegeren had a fake Vermeer that would fool the world. Despite claims of how he fooled the Nazis and helped the Dutch resistance, the activities of van Meegeren started well before the onset of World War II. In 1937 through a lawyer and friend, he had a painting brought to art critic and renowned Vermeer expert Abraham Bredius. His fake work, The Supper at Emmaus, was declared by Bredius to be a genuine Vermeer and one of his finest works.

In the aftermath of World War II with experts still unable to detect that the Vermeer paintings were fake, the post war Dutch Government charged him with conspiring with the enemy. The authorities had been alerted to and investigated his involvement in wartime art transactions with high ranking Nazis. So rather than be seen as a traitor, than a producer of fake paintings, van Meegeren confessed. His downfall came from one simple transaction selling to Hermann Goring. This was completed via a third party and he seemingly profited from the Nazi hierarchy, from what was at the time believed to be, an original Vermeer painting of the Woman Taken in Adultery, considered a Dutch national treasure. At his trial van Meegeren confessed to selling Goring a painting but that painting was a fake that he produced. His defence was that he did not conspire to aid the Nazis, but rather sold them a worthless fake and that he had traded the fake for approximately one hundred and twenty seven Dutch works of art. Which would have otherwise stayed with the Nazis in Germany. He would later argue at his trial that he was not a traitor, but a patriot, who used his talent for the good of the country.

The unique paints used by van Meegeren to imitate the Vermeer techniques were used as evidence at his trial and under police supervision he painted a new Vermeer fake of, Jesus Among the Doctors. Subsequently, the charge of conspiring with the enemy was dropped but van Meegeren was found guilty of the lesser charge of forgery. Only a month after the trial van Meegeren died of heart disease at the age of only fifty eight. Ultimately, his fame rose more from the fact that his case encompassed a world war and the use of his talents to save national treasures, than the quality of the actual fake paintings.

Chapter 7
Private Collectors, the Royal Collection and Art Money

Private Collectors

Private collectors of art and antiquities show both the good and the bad of the art world. In mitigation private collectors vary in size and wealth and can range from individuals, some famous in other fields, families, companies and the rulers of certain nations. The art and to a lesser extent antiquities, which are more often in museums due to ongoing conservation needs, is generally kept in their homes, office buildings or on loan to a commercial gallery or a museum. The primary concerns for the private collector should be buying art with a properly established provenance, taking the necessary conservation measures, physically protecting it and having proper insurance. And lending of the art in a methodical fashion to ensure its safe return from any commercial gallery or museum. Historically, when the collector is searching for the one key piece of art, that is when they are at their most vulnerable. However, when that legitimate flagship collection piece is finally acquired, a-game level security does not always follow.

The home of the private collector is burgled because of the owners simple neglect. Proper security systems and insurance are required to manage, protect and track the art as if it was on loan in a high profile museum exhibition. This process can begin by careful and full documentation of a private collection by using, for example, the aforementioned provenance checklist. This will include establishing the current market value for all the art in a collection and art insurers can provide valuable information to the private collector on how best to conduct general management of their collection. Next are the serious considerations of security for the location of the collection. If a collection is, in the main, in the home of the collector, appropriate physical security measures must be implemented. These could include integrated building alarm and CCTV systems, motion sensors, appropriate reinforced display casing or protective glass which in turn will be monitored with a glass (shaker) alarm. Depending on the quantity of the collection, in conjunction with the commensurate alarm system, the collector may need someone to monitor this system on a regular basis. Additionally, if the collector has an extremely valuable piece then consideration for deposit box style storage or a secret safe in their home, should be considered a priority.

The private collector is well known for their regular loans to commercial galleries and particularly museums. Where a certain painting belonging to a private collector can be a much sought after work for a particular high profile exhibition. Including already curated exhibitions that move from museum to museum. When the collector is lending, they must ensure the artwork is resilient enough to withstand travel and that they are happy with the museums insurance cover and what security arrangements will be in place. For the private collector theft or even damage of loaned art is a huge risk. There is first the reluctance of many collectors for insurance, then the risk of a museum having insurance cover and a contract with the collector that is inadequate for the artworks value, as well as a lack of due diligence in security matters and transportation. However, there are many private collectors who actively look to loan some of their most valued art for extensive periods. This is because their name is never revealed to the visiting public and the museum provides both insurance and security measures that would otherwise involve huge expenditure, over long periods, for the collector. That provides a benefit for both collector and museum, as well as art that would otherwise not be seen by the general public. However, for both planning and logistics, it can be argued that this is not the desired, or indeed sensible way forward, for the future security of art owned by the private collector.

Royal Collection

Possibly the most famous private collector in the world is King Charles III in the UK. Parts of the Royal Collection can, at various times and in various locations, be viewed by the public. Its upkeep is funded by the UK taxpayer and the King is described as the custodian of the collection. The collection is spread around all the royal palaces and on loan to museums and galleries all over the UK. However, most of the collection cannot be viewed by the public and for all intents and purposes is therefore, very much a private collection. It is the biggest art collection in the world and has been accumulated over some 400 years. It has over 1 million items and is said to be worth around £10 billion. It is the envy of the entire art world and a significant attraction to art historians, curators and dealers. The collection was started by Charles I who began a mass collecting programme and who laid the foundations for the Royal Collection. It was then significantly added to by George IV and Queen Victoria.

The Royal Collection is made up of sculptures, drawings (including one of the largest archives of Leonardo da Vinci drawings in the world) and some 7,000 paintings. Paintings include those of Vermeer, Rembrandt, Canaletto and a recently discovered Caravaggio painting. It was presumed lost but found in a cupboard at Hampton Court, and now valued at £50 million and is now a signature piece of the Royal Collection. The biggest asset in the collection are obviously the Crown Jewels valued at £5 billion.

The collection is used to display to visiting heads of state, of which there are two every year, and other dignitaries to effectively showcase Great Britain PLC. To do this the head of the collection will liaise with the Keeper (head librarian) of the collection who is based in the Round Tower at Windsor Castle. Together they draw up a list of objects relevant to the country of those people visiting. For example, Barak Obama and wife Michelle were shown a 1st edition of the book Birds of America valued at £11 million. This then poses the question of how many of the foreign artworks shown, should not be in the possession of the Royal Collection, but rather those visiting countries themselves.

It has one of the most extensive collections of Faberge objects anywhere in the world. It includes six hundred Faberge items, including some famous eggs. Some of the objects were initially gifts from Faberge to Russian royalty. This Faberge collection within the Royal Collection was started with a commission made by Edward VII as a Christmas present to his wife Alexandria, during the 1900s. The commission was a collection of carved hardstone, semi-precious, figures of animals that lived on the royal farm on the Sandringham estate. The most iconic Faberge object in the collection is the bejewelled mosaic easter egg. It was originally a present from Nicholas II to his wife and contained a further jewel inside showing images of their children. It is described as a masterpiece of latticework of platinum, inset with different precious stones. It was then bought by his cousin George V in 1933 for £250 around £19 million today and was subsequently given to the Queen Elizabeth II.

In recent times the late Queen Elizabeth II made some surprising purchases for the collection. In 2012 she bought four Andy Warhol paintings of herself. It is not known how much was paid, but similar works of popular culture celebrities have sold for as much as $80 million.

The Royal Collection, however, has not been immune to fraudulent activity. In 2019 the then Prince Charles, agreed to take on loan seventeen paintings from billionaire James Stunt, the ex-husband of former Formula 1 chief Bernie Ecclestone's daughter. They were hung in Dumfries house in Scotland, home to the princes foundation and a visitor attraction. They were collectively estimated to be worth £200 million. However, it was discovered that four of the paintings were forgeries, a Monet and a Picasso, and it has been suggested by art experts that they were so very obviously forged paintings. They were painted by an American art forger Tony Tetro who admitted creating the forged artwork, but James Stunt denied any wrongdoing on his part. The then Prince Charles unsurprisingly immediately removed and returned all the paintings. Thus avoiding further embarrassment, not just to the royal family, but for the integrity of the entire royal collection.

Art Money

There is much secrecy in the art world regarding who owns what. In many exhibitions, even those not of the highest calibre, you will see art that has been loaned. Despite all the details given about the actual painting, unless loaned by a commercial gallery or museum, it more often than not lists the owner as, Private Collection, no names are present. Serious private collectors in the Middle East are rivalled by those in Russia, China and India and competition for those signature pieces is fierce. As a result there have been increasing levels of secrecy regarding actual ownership. However, the art world is fairly confident that Qatar is the country sitting on the best treasure chest of artwork, at this moment in time.

As a result of extreme interest from private buyers in the Middle East prices for paintings, in particular, are becoming more and more excessive. As a result of the vast amounts being paid it creates incredible instability in the art markets. In the sense of inflationary activity in the art market concerning Middle East buyers, a parallel can be made with elite level sport as well as the money being spent to attract events to the region. This has already started by way of a FIFA World Cup in 2022, high profile professional boxing in Saudi Arabia, Formula 1 racing in the region, bids for staging the Americas Cup and most recently, the LIV Golf events offering huge prize money.

Similarly, the UAE has launched a serious national art project. They have allegedly paid $0.5 billion to lease the Louvre name for thirty years, for the newly built Louvre Abu Dhabi. With another $0.75 billion to loan three hundred art works from them, with a similar deal struck with the Guggenheim Museum in New York. This is important because museums tend to be known by a feature work, thirty to thirty-five percent of people who visit the Louvre only go there to see the Mona Lisa. They come through a separate entrance they queue in a separate line, they see the Mona Lisa and then leave and remember, this is one of the great museums in the world with a vast and impressive collection, not just home to the Mona Lisa. It is rumoured the aforementioned Salvator Mundi will be its signature piece.

The storage methods of artwork have also been in the spotlight in recent years, with the advent of Freeports and the economic and privacy advantages they provide, legally. Allegedly eighty percent of all the worlds art is in storage at any one time. A lot of art buyers are only interested in a profit when they sell so storage that is safe and secure is important to their plans. Artwork that is stored in Freeports also attracts no tax or related business issues. Freeports have been around since the late nineteenth century. Originally created to store grain and other products used in international trade, they have the ability to store assets longer term without attracting tax whilst in transit. This is seen as beneficial to governments, traders and consumers alike. In terms of a painting, for example, if someone buys one in New York for $50 million it might attract tax in the region of $4-5 million. However, if it is immediately moved to a Freeport that tax bill disappears. Until the owner moves it to their residence, somewhere in Manhattan!

There are around fifteen to twenty Freeports in the world and a handful of these are major ones. They have the floor space of about thirty six NFL pitches and sixty percent of them are full of art and antiquity of one description or another. They are technically not part of the country in which they are situated. They are generally situated next to airport runways. So a high end art collector can land in a private jet, take a painting out of the jet, deposit it in the freeport and then re-board the jet and just leave. However, there is never any record of the person ever arriving and making a deposit. No name, no date, no time and no deposit details. Perfect, not just for tax avoidance, but for art purchased using criminal funds or art that has been stolen in another jurisdiction, in the last twenty four hours. All in all extremely unhelpful for any subsequent law enforcement investigations or chances of recovery.

Geneva Freeport is a warehouse complex in Switzerland, used for the storage of art, valuables and other collectibles. It is the oldest and largest freeport facility in the world and the one with the most stored artwork, with forty percent of its stored assets being art. Which is estimated as 1.1 million artworks, with an estimated value of US$100 billion. This freeport became the preferred storage facility for the international elite due to the capacity of Switzerland's storage and customs laws. It has since come under scrutiny for its complicity in the looted antiquities trade and money laundering schemes. The facility's holdings, especially those possibly related to tax avoidance, have been subject to increasingly greater scrutiny. In reality, whether it be the Geneva freeport or any other the storage of art is very likely to increase in the future, not decline.

SECURITY

Chapter 1
Museum Security

This chapter will not focus on specific details about museum security, but rather on the curator versus security debate. As well as a generic overview of what basic planning and risk management measures should be in place for any museum, which would also be applicable to the larger commercial gallery. Many of the same security challenges present themselves for all museums, but any security measures need to be tailored made for them to be effective. That means they must be present in any overarching security strategy as well as its day to day operations. In recent years outside of university museums, such as the Fitzwilliam in Cambridge, most museums would have listed education as down on their list of organisational priorities. Nowadays museums due to the need for inclusion and to assert greater justification for themselves and the collections they hold, would now describe themselves as centres for public learning.

Museum visitors need to be able to see art and antiquities in a safe and tranquil environment. However, a difficult balance must be struck between keeping the collection as safe as possible and still granting public access to them. Otherwise a museum can develop a fortress mentality and ultimately visitors cannot properly tour a museum with the freedom a collection would deserve. Bottom line, if you want to give public access to original and famous artwork there will always be a risk. They are two key contradictions, curator versus security, which must somehow meet on mutual ground. It can be argued that in most museums the curator wins and there is no mutual ground achieved or even sort. A visible museum security presence can cause some visitors to feel that they are being watched too closely as they move around a museum. But with the proper training and deployment, security personnel can do their job without impeding visitor enjoyment.

In most cases the curator winning should still not affect museum security as long as six important security factors are applied, this being; a security strategy, constant risk assessment of the collection followed by the required risk mitigation, regular museum documentation dip-sampling, better communication between operational and curatorial staff and training for non-security staff, that lessons have been learned from previous incidents and senior museum management practice a risk aware culture and are prepared to financially invest in it. The reality is this rarely happens despite the constant vulnerability to damaging thefts.

Security Strategy

Security in museums will effectively follow most security frameworks but should be tailored made, what any strategy will highlight is the need for planning and emergency response because the main concern for any museum will be fire. This is discussed at length in that particular chapter in this section. Strategy must include key elements such as a periodic security survey of the museum building and its collection. In addition to normal operations, planning should be thorough for exhibitions or loaned art and antiquities which may include a jewel in the crown showpiece artwork. Museum security needs a clear and objective infrastructure designed so the Visitor Services department can function hand in hand with security personnel, with everyone following procedures and protocols.

An acute awareness of insider theft should be a priority because it is difficult to prevent and depending on the role of the thief at the museum, may take years to detect. Insider theft is very difficult to detect, quantify and mitigate because it involves human activities and not the fixed characteristics of a building or the people visiting it. Employee evaluation should include reviews of recruitment procedures and ongoing periodic background security checks. Any strategy would also need to include registration and monitoring of visitors/academics accessing the collection in departments behind closed doors.

Gallery attendants should have an actual interest in the art and antiquities they are employed to oversee not just be there for the pay cheque. Security staff should be licensed for both CCTV and visitor supervision which should include conflict management training. Security personnel should work primarily from the security suite with the monitoring of CCTV being the basis of all operational activity. For example, alerting attendants when a visitor touches a painting or is leaning on an alarmed display case. Foot security can then simultaneously move around assessing risk and provide an immediate response if an incident not seen on CCTV occurs. In museums a key element of the operational framework is the Duty Manager system, who are responsible for any incident response, security or otherwise, including medical emergencies.

Risk Assessment and Mitigation

Absolutely everyone who works at a museum, whether they are senior management, a curator, a gallery attendant or even work in the museum cafe, has a responsibility for security because once the artwork is gone it may never be recovered. They are the extra eyes and ears of the security department. Policies and procedures vary too broadly between museums and generic government advice is not always followed as well as it should be. This is fact. However, the first rule of museum security is we do not talk about security even between museum security managers, therefore comparisons in best practice is rarely made and bad practice never revealed, so as to be rectified. A holistic approach to museum security is essential, with a layered approach and each risk assessed on its own merits using available resources with any individual or collective issues then reported to the security manager and immediately resolved. This may involve a gallery or museum closure depending on the issue. For example, a defective display case, faulty alarm(s) or a painting discovered with insufficient security by way of its hanging screws/brackets. Nowadays museum security needs to combine high-tech with low-tech security measures, although they should always start with the nuts and bolts such as anchoring works to immovable objects correctly.

For the future, there could be two new security options. Recent security advances in crowded public places has been the SPOT programme known as Screening Passengers by Observation Techniques. A tactic originally devised by airport security management. Basically a racially neutral observation baseline to identify persons in airports exhibiting behaviours outside of the norm. Using a baseline set of behaviours for a particular location, such as a museum, and then observing those people whose behaviour is outside of that baseline. Electronic tracking devices will also be key. This needs to be undertaken within a security strategy and the technology may be the future of art theft prevention. Deploying GPS technology to protect art by the careful secretion of GPS onto a painting, sculpture or antiquity being the main challenge and it will come at a financial cost. Similarly, there are a number of measures that a museum security manager can take at little or no cost to their budget. These can include engagement of all staff of a museum and gallery staff in identifying threats and being vigilant in enforcing security measures such as door access usage by those issued cards, tailgating by those not and consistent

ID badge display. However, this will only materialise if supported by senior management within a positive security culture.

Documentation Sampling

This is one of the most important areas in museum security and emergency planning/response and yet another area neglected by many. Documentation is the record of all art and antiquities owned or on-loan by a museum for which nationally required, tailor made software, is advised be used as best practice. Imagine a museum, for example, owning two million items. A million of which are kept in the basement reserve at any one time so there should, by design, be an absolute need for available and accurate information regarding their location at any given time. Museum items are also moved from display or the reserve for conservation. So when a museum location or display case is attended after consulting museum documentation software, the art or antiquity should indeed be at that location. Whether it be in the display case or on the wall, removed for conservation or safely stored in the reserve.

The beauty of periodic documentation dip-sampling, for example, is that thirty items out of one million can be checked by security attending thirty locations in the museum over a couple of days. If there is but one item not where it should be that is great cause for concern, as the artwork could be a priceless piece. Documentation dip-sampling assures that staff are making sure that when items are moved they are properly documented. This helps in internal thefts going unnoticed for long periods, especially when a collection is vast.

Communication and Training

This simple human activity is invisible a lot of the time in museums. Just ask anyone you know who works in one. To be successful in the security of museum assets curatorial and security staff need to have regular communication. This should take place regularly and especially during any new artwork acquisition, loan or exhibition. Security aspects must be discussed and a plan mutually agreed and more importantly stuck with. From here regular briefings for both security staff and gallery attendants relating to the loaned artwork and any newly furnished exhibition gallery. This is after all just basic risk management on a daily basis with the communication part added. Any communication regarding an artwork must also be disseminated to other relevant departments in the museum making sure there are no gaps in the agreed procedures to keep everything safe. Regular in-house training of all non-security staff is needed so they feel vested in any security programme, so when an incident does occur those staff feel confident enough to take the initial steps to get a response moving. Training should be specific, relevant and bite-size, so it can be remembered by staff under pressure and for it to be successful, provided regularly and repetitiously.

Learning Lessons

When a museum has been subject to a famous theft of art which may never be recovered, such as those at Isabella Stewart Gardner Museum in 1990, or subject to a theft which hurts specific areas of their collection, such as the estimated thirty million pound theft of Chinese jade from the Fitzwilliam Museum Cambridge in 2012, lessons must be learnt. This is absolutely crucial when it concerns art and antiquities and indeed lessons can be learnt. When any high profile theft occurs it becomes instant media headlines and so to unfortunately for whatever museum involved, does the glaring security lapses that allow a vast majority of these thefts to happen.

No detailed specifics are ever revealed by the museums concerned and neither as you would expect, do investigating law enforcement agencies reveal anything of importance. However, by reading details in the press of the simplicity of the theft, more often than not, it is not difficult to work out that something went seriously wrong with security and the term negligent immediately comes to mind.

Regardless of art insurance or eventual recovery, these thefts are damaging to museums. Because much like a domestic burglary theft statistics show that once you have been a victim you are vulnerable to it happening again, committed by the same thief. The thief is confident they can break in again because they know the museum vulnerabilities and they are happy to hedge their bets that the museum has not tightened up measures completely or the museum thinks the burglar has got what they wanted and not be back again. Learning a lesson, albeit a costly one, always presents an opportunity to review things and tighten up procedures or better still, go back to basics and have a root and branch overhaul of security.

Management Risk

A risk aware culture at museums must come in the first instance from senior management, otherwise it will not filter down through the organisation and will never be taken seriously by staff. Budgetary constraints and decisions made by museum directors, who by design have backgrounds in curating, and therefore seem to purvey a sense of it will not happen at their museum and this has an obvious detrimental effect on security. Only after a loss has been incurred and the tragedy of the piece involved does the security manager start to be heard. Most of the above measures come at zero cost to museum senior management but has to be set up within the right culture, a culture which will only work if it comes from the very top. When staff know without any doubt they also have a responsibility for security and that any detrimental actions by them will have consequences, you will be surprised how a quality security culture will indeed rise within a museum, gain momentum and most importantly, become the norm.

Chapter 2
Law Enforcement

When theft happens law enforcement and government agencies, if relevant, should be notified as well as any private art loss registries. Museums and commercial galleries are often hesitant to publicise a theft, fearing disclosure will highlight security deficiencies and will dissuade collectors from lending. The reality is that recoveries are still rare and limited. The Federal Bureau of Investigation (FBI) has suggested only ten percent of stolen art and antiquities worldwide is ever recovered. In those few instances where a reward is agreed by all parties concerned to be offered, it does not always entice those with knowledge of the theft to come forward. Following the theft from the Isabella Stewart Gardner Museum, it offered $5 million for information resulting in the recovery of works, but as of 2022 they are still yet to pay out that reward.

Most countries have no dedicated art police as well as previous and current law enforcement policy for the security of art and antiquities, patchy. When news of stolen artwork emerges and police become involved hardly any reference is made as to whether dedicated art theft officers are being used to investigate the case. This is because more often, they are not. Governments or police commanders generally consider art crime not of sufficient severity to warrant a department all of its own. This may have some valid merit and reasoning on their part when we consider the available related crime figures and data, as alluded to in the previous chapter. To begin with, as a result of sparse initial intelligence data and before any complaint of a crime is even made, law enforcement agencies will not start to try and form an understanding of the problem or commit any real resources to it.

To be fair, law enforcement agencies worldwide have a difficult remit and this is always exacerbated with the need to prioritise resources and deal with unexpected incidents that require the immediate allocation of human resources. The bottom line in relation to police art and antiquities theft is that the recovery rate remains low because to both recover stolen art and to successfully prosecute is rare. However, the greatest amount of data and subsequent analysis comes from these solved cases, so it becomes understandable that limited data is available on art crime. Two key policy areas that would help decrease art crime is prevention and punishment and from these it has been suggested quality international policy for both art and antiquities can be formulated. However, to succeed in this, international cooperation must function at a high level. Whether this can be achieved remains to be seen with different competing and unexpected domestic issues and priorities for law enforcement agencies in culturally different countries.

Law Enforcement Agencies

So at this point in trying to understand the work of law enforcement with the theft of art and antiquities, we can only look at some of those countries with the more successful art theft departments. A first step has been their knowledge and experience gained in the actual investigation of art crime starting with their intelligence databases. This data has been developed over a number of years, interpreting art crime and locating geographical areas of high risk. Especially important in those databases has been the input of countries that can be defined as producers of art and antiquities such as Egypt, Peru, Italy and the Netherlands which is then exchanged with all the international law enforcement agencies.

The Carabinieri Division for the Protection of Cultural Heritage in Italy stands as the oldest and largest of art crime departments in the world. The department comprises four different sections: archaeological sites, antiquity dealing, fake art and theft of contemporary art. It has been by far the most successful art investigation department in the world, with over 300 full time officers. However, Italy does report more stolen art each year than any other country. The Carabinieri art department has been active in Iraq and Afghanistan and is sufficiently large and well-funded to undertake policing at the designated at-risk archaeological sites, with a select worldwide remit.

The Metropolitan Police Art and Antiques Unit is a branch of the Metropolitan Police based in New Scotland Yard in London. The purpose of the unit is to investigate art theft, illegal art smuggling, fake art and document forgery with the UK art market being the second largest in the world. However, the jurisdiction of the unit only covers London and the numerous art thefts outside of London are investigated by provincial police with no special training in art crime. Over the years the unit has been subject to budget cuts and disbandment but has been recently reformed. To counter a lack of funding, the unit developed new policies, such as a program in which art world specialists work for several days each month assisting police officers with ongoing investigations. Antiquities seized by the unit in 2002 were recently repatriated to Afghanistan.

The FBI Art Crime Team features several dedicated agents supported by special trial attorneys for prosecutions. The FBI has had remarkable success in this capacity, despite the fact that a relatively small number of art thefts actually occur in the United States. Rather, the United States with such a large scope as an art market serves as a preferred venue to sell stolen art. For this reason the FBI has helped other countries recover their stolen art and has participated in numerous undercover sting operations in collaboration with foreign law enforcement agencies.

The KLPD is the art crime unit of the Netherlands. It represents one of the new faces in international art crime law enforcement. Consisting of only a few agents including the only one in the Netherlands with experience and expertise in investigating art crime. The team was founded when it became clear that art crime was extending into the higher levels of organized crime within their jurisdiction, the government then deemed art crime an issue of national importance.

Interpol

The International Criminal Police Organization, commonly known as Interpol, is an international organisation that facilitates worldwide police cooperation. Contrary to popular belief Interpol is in itself, not a law enforcement agency. Headquartered in Lyon France it is the world's largest international police organization, with seven regional bureaus worldwide and smaller national bureaus in all one hundred and ninety five member states. Interpol provides investigative support, expertise and training to law enforcement agencies worldwide. Its broad mandate covers virtually every kind of crime and the agency also facilitates cooperation among national law enforcement institutions, through criminal databases and communications networks. Interpol's Stolen Works of Art Department acts as an information gathering point for world art law enforcement and ranks art crime as the fourth highest grossing criminal trade, only behind drugs, arms and human trafficking.

Data

Several law enforcement agencies along with Interpol have integrated digital technology and digitisation into their investigative process, to help recover stolen or missing art and antiquities. The Carabinieri has been at the forefront of utilising databases to help deter the trafficking of art and cultural heritage objects. One of the best known databases of the Carabinieri is the one named Leonardo. Officially integrated in 1992, it is the biggest art database in the world and contains the names and photographs of well over six million registered works of art. Of those over one million are classified as stolen, missing, illegally excavated or smuggled. Leonardo has a high recovery record and by 2014 the Carabinieri had recovered 137000 works, with an estimated value of over £400 million.

Closely associated with Leonardo is the Interpol stolen works of art database with the goal of centralising information about stolen items and disseminating that information globally, within law enforcement agencies. The database contains in excess of 45000 records from one hundred and twenty-nine different countries. It has successfully returned 2800 items since 1995. The data programme is available to law enforcement personnel through the secure Interpol communications systems and has since been made available to authorised members of the public. Users from over eighty-eight countries now have access to the database. In 2012 Interpol and the Carabinieri launched the Protection System for Cultural Heritage (PSYCHE) to effectively combine the collective knowledge of the two agencies. It allows for automatic transfer of queries to the Italian Leonardo database so those results can be analysed and reassessed by that system. This is in itself an indication that not all systems were or have been designed to be integrated from the outset, perhaps not just for data logistic reasons but also the absence of data protection legislation worldwide. The

United States being a prime example of this, despite the important successes of the FBI.

The Future

The relationship between law enforcement and art crime in the future still remains uncertain. With the aforementioned law enforcement issues over lack of reporting of art theft, lack of intelligence, the will to fund art crime departments, human resources, domestic priorities and unexpected incidents such as terrorism, it seems that incremental steps only, will continue to be made. However, an international policy change may assist in those incremental steps to a greater extent. An international policy would involve the establishment of national teams to establish and evaluate their own degree of risk, but not just law enforcement based. Any policy formulation will include museums, churches, private collectors, insurers, auction houses, art dealers, government agencies and international organisations such as the United Nations Educational, Scientific and Cultural Organisation (UNESCO).

Effectively, there must be more scope for the provenance of all art and antiquities, increased border controls when art and antiquities are moved internationally, registration of artwork on as many databases as possible and most importantly the reporting of theft when it occurs. However, much of this goes against the current activities and desires of those same people who like what they own to remain private or not to be revealed once it is stolen or goes missing. These collective policy measures will not necessarily represent the definitive solution. A new increased international policy may not be appropriate for some countries due to the state of their internal affairs, such as those in South America, Africa and the Middle East. However, it is the simplest way to evaluate and exert control. A structurally basic policy, that may be adopted to fit the needs of individual nations and underscores the UNESCO

ART CRIME AND SECURITY

philosophy of prohibiting and preventing the illicit import, export and transfer of ownership of cultural property. Ultimately, the battle against art crime by law enforcement agencies can only be won with unconditional international cooperation and data flow.

Chapter 3
Emergency Planning and Response for Art

One of the most crucial areas for security is in emergencies concerning the preservation of art and antiquities in the commercial gallery, museum and for those with a large private collection. It applies to a range of threats which vary in type and magnitude including fire, flood, accidental and criminal damage, bomb threats and theft. Underpinning this must be an emergency plan and if a large gallery or museum, business continuity considerations. As in any other business, emergency planning should be covered by policy and procedures including security and risk management measures, in conjunction with a salvage operation. The main areas highlighted in this chapter are specific to security and emergency planning for art and antiquities, but which are still prepared under the basic framework of any crisis management and business continuity plan, used by any other organisation. Crucial to this, is the salvage of art and antiquities whether they be destroyed, damaged, needing conservation or restoration work or indeed recovered intact. Security teams should be responsible for all art and antiquities, whether in a collection or not and whether located at the temporary emergency location or other permanent storage facility. Security management will advise the senior response team on the required security measures during an emergency. In a larger emergency they will advise on whether all or part of a location must be closed and will liaise directly with the emergency services, if or when they are involved. Any security management team and its staff would work in conjunction with three other key teams in an emergency. The senior (management) response team, salvage and documentation (conservation) team and the business continuity (communications and logistics) team, when that phase is reached.

Incident Categories

Minor (Category 3)

Can be described as actual physical damage, water leaks, extreme high or lows of humidity and pest infestation causing minor damage to individual art and antiquities or a collection. This would require a consultation regarding closure of the effected commercial gallery or specific museum area.

Moderate (Category 2)

Can be described as burst pipes, a small fire, accidental major physical damage or criminal damage to individual art and antiquities or a collection. This would require the immediate closure of the effected commercial gallery or museum area.

Major (Category 1)

Can be described as fire, flood, bomb threat/terrorism and theft events. Requires the immediate closure of the entire commercial gallery or museum.

Salvage

After the obvious consideration of human life and personal property for visitors and staff to a commercial gallery or museum, a salvage operation of the relevant art and antiquities is a priority for any emergency planning procedures that are then activated. The commercial galley or museum concerned with be in possession of salvage lists of art and antiquities that should take priority over other museum art in any salvage operation and these lists will be highly restricted documents, for obvious theft prevention reasons. The value put on the art in these lists by the commercial gallery or museum will be considered in terms of cultural, reputational or financial importance. Any salvage operation aims to protect individual art, antiquities or collections to prevent further damage and salvage must be undertaken immediately and methodically. This often means simple removal to a safe environment where any subsequent conservation or restoration work is then undertaken.

Salvage Priority Lists

Salvage priority lists are an accreditation requirement by the UK Arts Council for most museums and would indicate best practice for the commercial gallery and those with large private collections. For those responsible, agreeing priorities in advance helps to avoid poor decision making during an emergency. Art and antiquities on these lists may be retrieved quickly from the scene by the emergency services before anyone else has access to the site. If these key items are impossible to move quickly then they can be made a priority for protective measures in situ, such as raising the item from the ground and covering with a protective sheet.

      A priority list must be prepared in advance by curators, gallery owners or private collectors. Factors affecting their choices on those lists will include uniqueness, rarity or iconic status, monetary or cultural value, art and antiquities particularly fragile or vulnerable to damage, academic research value and just as important for the museum, art that is on loan.

A museum in particular, due to exhibitions and private collectors loaning vast amounts of art each year or museums holding art in lieu of inheritance tax allocated across museums by government, should not differentiate between its own collection and loans when setting salvage priorities. This in any case is explicitly stated in the UK government Museum Indemnity Scheme agreement. Importantly, where art and antiquities are on long term loan and included in priority salvage lists, the loan status must be recorded and highlighted within those priority lists, for insurance or government indemnity purposes.

Salvage Management and Documentation

Emergencies are unpredictable, so it may not be possible to salvage all art and antiquities on the priority list. In a museum emergency the appointed Salvage Manager will be continually advised by the appropriate curator or conservator or both. Then make the final decision on what is removed to safety first based on what salvage actions are possible at the time. For example, a high priority painting may be more vulnerable than an even more significant bronze sculpture which is in an extremely secure display case. So in this case the painting may be salvaged first, despite being of less importance to the museum.

Art and antiquities on any list during a salvage operation need to be properly documented when they are recovered, whether damaged or not. This ensures that the correct status of the artwork or collection is recorded for internal purposes and subsequent insurance/indemnity claims, including those moved out to a secondary location for safe keeping. Documentation also facilitates effective communication with the lenders regarding loan material. Further review of this documentation during the emergency and after, would continue to facilitate the best way forward. For example a painting on loan from a private collector is recovered undamaged but the collector would rather its immediate return until the museum is fully operational again. Or they may cancel the loan period immediately if they have concerns over its ongoing vulnerability.

Senior Response Team

The SRT, affectively the overall emergency management team should ensure that for the larger commercial gallery or museum, emergency preparedness is fully integrated into any future planning and development of a gallery or museum location, its facilities and operational activities, such as exhibitions. All staff involved in an emergency must understand that the SRT has authority in the final decision making process. Where art and antiquities are involved, individual staff such as curators in specialist areas, may have strong opinions during any salvage operation as to what should take priority regardless of any list. For those individuals or families with large private collections (unless the owners have some expertise in curating or conservation) good practice dictates they would have employed an art expert who has advised them on any salvage operation and a priority list. This person would likely be on a retainer and called in to act as an SRT equivalent and when needed, bring in their own team. With what we already know about private collectors, there are probably only a small percentage who will have planned for this, ultimately relying on insurance cover.

Pre-planning and Emergency Manual

A working group should be established to oversee all aspects of emergency planning and response in the commercial gallery or museum. A working group should meet regularly and periodically throughout the year or extraordinarily when required. A working group enables the most effective communication between the different parts of a large gallery or museum to inform and improve emergency preparedness measures. By distributing crucial knowledge within the group it is more resilient to staff changes and importantly, avoids an over-reliance on a few specialist individuals.

As with any other crisis and business continuity management, an Emergency Manual must exist. It must be a confidential and restricted document and only made available to relevant and authorised staff. Access to it should be controlled by security management and be available both physically and digitally. It should be reviewed on a regular basis by the working group and refined or updated as required. Any manual will mirror the standard framework for crisis and business continuity, which will not be explored here. Crucially, in relation to emergency planning and response for art, it will include the salvage priority list and salvage operation guidance. Finally, as with any other organisational response, staff training is extremely important but especially when it concerns art and antiquities. Where the ability to respond quickly and make decisions on items which may be the only ones in existence, is vital.

Chapter 4
Art and Insurance

Most of us would think art and insurance are inseparable partners, but like law enforcement activities and museum security there is still much left to be desired. As we have seen from past thefts, such as the Isabella Stewart Gardner Museum, no insurance provision can have serious long term consequences whilst other stolen art has been woefully underinsured. Art insurance generally comes under three main guises, insurance of art as a subsegment of home insurance, specialist art insurance which would cover art collections and antiquities provided for by the specialist arm of certain insurers and government indemnity schemes. All these options concentrate on both prevention and the protocols required to keep the art and antiquities safe. When thefts do occur the investigation and recovery process is often protracted. The insurance company, as you would expect, will do everything to recover the stolen work. Theft is much more prevalent in uninsured institutions and due to the remote or dangerous location of antiquities. Institutions such as churches do not have the resources to invest in risk mitigation. Whilst archaeological sites due to their sheer size, such as those in South America or cultural properties in conflict zones, such as those in the Middle East, remain an obstacle to any insurance ambitions.

Popular culture combined with poetic licence paint an unrealistic picture of art theft as a readily solvable crime with a daring recovery plot. For example the insurance investigator and the art thief narrative such as Renee Russo vs Pierce Brosnan in the Thomas Crown Affair (1999) Catherine Zeta Jones vs Sean Connery in Entrapment (1999) and the series The Last Panthers with Samantha Morton and John Hurt (2015). As you would expect in reality the process is very much that of law enforcement investigation, processes and procedures with insurers working closely alongside the authorities. Perhaps a reason in itself why owners, such as private collectors, choose not to insure art. While insurance claims can provide back the current value of a stolen work, we also know it offers no real heart felt consolation. As it can never equal the return of an item which more often than not, will be irreplaceable.

In addition to insurance for museums and private collectors, government art indemnity legislation exists in countries such as the US, Canada, Australia and the UK. These are very much concentrated on the display of special individual art or antiquities and museum exhibitions. For example, The UK Government Indemnity Scheme is an alternative to commercial insurance. It allows art and culturally important antiquities to be shown publicly which might not have been because the cost of insurance would have been too high. The scheme provides cost free indemnity cover for loss or damage when items are on short or long term loan. It encourages non-national museums to hold important exhibitions or add to existing collections and also allows those museums to borrow art and antiquities for study purposes. Importantly, any publicly accessible museum or institution is eligible to apply for this indemnity cover. The scheme currently saves museums and galleries around £20 million a year.

Art insurance away from government indemnity, of which loses are clearly covered by the taxpayer, is a profitable business. Statistics wise the risk loss ratio is currently very much in favour of the insurers, with the huge sums paid to insure art and antiquities far outweighing their pay outs as a result of theft. This is surprising as regards to what has already been discussed but might be an indication of two things. First, that there is a very large amount of art and antiquities out there in the world owned by various museums and individuals and it is insured, maybe of medium value and not of cultural significance and therefore not subject to theft and subsequent media attention. Second, some of the more famous art and antiquities remains uninsured maybe due to the extreme privacy of the owner, the cost to insure it and its scarcity alongside cultural significance. Unfortunately, not all art and antiquities belong to their nation of origin but to private collectors and other museums and galleries, so their adequate protection is not always guaranteed.

Each insurer reports data differently and not all reported claims enter the public domain. As prices in the art market continue to rise insurance rates have remained reasonable. As long as paid losses do not exceed premiums received and competition between insurance companies continues, it is anticipated that current insurance market conditions for art and antiquities will remain steady. In relation to theft this accounts for only one of the risks, physical dangers such as fire, flooding, accidental damage and pest infestation remain on the agenda of insurers.

Insured or indemnified art and antiquities is one where risks have been evaluated. Art and antiquities are stored, displayed or reside in many different locations each posing different risks to its safety. As previously mentioned in the museum security chapter, risk assessment provides the first step in any insurance cover decision by the insurer and assessment of buildings is the starting point. The geographical location, exterior perimeter protection and lighting, gallery configuration, CCTV and alarm systems. Then actual security personnel and other employees with access to the collection, along with the requirement for security checks on those people. All these would apply to the domestic residence or office of private collectors and all their personal staff and employees.

Clearly the display of art and antiquities can increase or reduce the potential for theft. How a painting was affixed to a wall or an antiquity anchored to its stand are very important when a claim is activated. Should a theft occur proper documentation of art will ease the search and recovery process, whilst all museums should be using documentation software alongside standardised national procedures as a twin process. This is because museums on average display only five percent of their permanent collections, with the remaining ninety-five percent housed in on-site and off-site facilities, some allowing for multiple art from a single collection to be dispersed throughout that facility. Without proper documentation art and antiquities are at risk of theft. Unlike in the movies, insurers undertake the process much the same as with any other claim. Insurance companies deploy insurance adjusters to investigate the loss, with most fine art adjusters being independent with some art expertise employed by insurers. They sometimes employ investigators with a police background but not necessarily in art, as the investigative process is much the same as in any crime. You just need an investigator who is like a dog with a bone, has attention to detail and is process aware. The investigator and adjustor then collaborate presenting a final report to the insurer.

Most losses with the exception of those resulting from theft are partial losses and therefore partial claims with adjusted payments made. For example, if a painting is subject to accidental water damage whereby a section may require relining the insurer only then compensates for that. However, if it is the result of a burglary whereby the thief was interrupted and only damage is caused to the painting, the process becomes more specific. First, the insurance company need to determine the current market value of the painting by getting an updated valuation by an art expert.

Then a conservator will attempt to restore the painting to its former condition. The work will again be assessed for its value and whether there is a loss due to the repair. The insurer will then pay for any differential loss in the value of the painting from its current market value as well as the cost of repair, which may be quite extensive and time consuming.

Potential for theft or damage increases when art and antiquities are in transit. The procedures should include the use of recognised art transport companies along with an approved road route, as well as an alternative option. With some high value shipments requiring staff from the loanee to be on board the shipping vehicle or in following cars, or if shipping from abroad, accompanying the art on any cargo plane. Insurers would also ask the owner to get an updated art expert valuation to reflect current market values and not the purchase price. This should be done in conjunction with the lender and the insurance document should reflect this. Insurers, as well as those government officials authorising indemnity cover, should have already reviewed the policies and procedures for art loan security at the lending museum before, facilitating its safe transition from vehicle to building.

REPATRIATION AND RECOVERY

Chapter 1
Office of Strategic Services File – 1945

TOP SECRET

THIRD REICH PLUNDER

Information on Nazi Stolen
Art Operations

Restricted Document

Introduction

The Nazi plunder was the stealing of art and other items which occurred as a result of the organised looting of various European countries, during the time of the Third Reich. Art and antiquities were a major preoccupation of the Nazi elite and between 1935 to 1945 Hitler spent 163 million Reichsmark on artwork, making him technically the greatest art buyer of all time. In addition to gold and jewellery, the Nazis stole about 5 million pieces of art. Not just from the Jewish people but from museums, universities and churches, utilising their position of power to amass art for both private and public benefit.

These activities were undertaken by agents who acted on behalf of the ruling Nazi party of Germany, officially the National Socialist German Workers Party (NSDAP) a far right political party active from 1920-1945. The looting of Jewish property in all its forms, was a key part of the Holocaust. Kunstschutz (art protection) was the German term for the principle of preserving cultural heritage and artworks during armed conflict especially during World War I and World War II, with the stated aim of protecting the enemy art and returning it after the end of hostilities. In no aspect whatsoever was this policy ever activated by the Nazi regime. It was mere window dressing rhetoric, used between the wars to counter civil protest and counterbalance any World War I destruction. It would therefore redeem itself in the eyes of international agencies, whilst regaining its image as a land of culture and respecter of heritage.

The plundering was carried out from 1933, beginning with the seizure of the property of German Jews and continued until the end of the war. Most of the art was stolen during the war and also included gold, silver, currency and cultural items of great significance, including religious treasures and books. Their ultimate aim was to exile or murder their victims via the concentration camps and steal their worldly possessions. Art collections from prominent Jewish families including the Rothschilds, Rosenberg's, Goudstikkers and the Schloss family were targeted because of their significant value. By the end of the war, the Third Reich had amassed hundreds of thousands of cultural objects.

Many of these items were recovered by personnel of the Monuments, Fine Arts and Archives department (MFAA) commonly known as the Monuments Men, on behalf of the Allied Forces a short time after German surrender, with many of them still missing. A subsequent international governmental effort, led by the Allies, to identify Nazi plunder still unaccounted for is underway. With the ultimate aim of returning the items to their rightful owners, their families or their respective countries. How successful this will be cannot be predicted nor can the timescale. Intelligence indicates many of these artworks will never be recovered and returned.

Art Looting Investigation Unit (ALIU)

The unit was created in 1944 by the Roberts Commission, led by Owen Roberts an Associate Justice of the United States Supreme Court, to focus on works of cultural value during the war. At the request of Justice Roberts, Mr William J. Donovan head of the Office of Strategic Services (OSS) created the ALIU within and under the direct control of the OSS, with a remit to report to the Roberts Commission. The terms of reference for the ALIU was to collect information on the looting, confiscation and transfer of cultural objects by Nazi Germany. The collaborators, both individuals and organisations involved, the restitution of property and ultimately the prosecution of those responsible. This is effectively the intelligence arm of the ongoing fieldwork of the MFAA since 1943.

ALIU – Reports and Indexes

The ALIU reports detail the networks of Nazi officials, art dealers and individuals involved in the Third Reich policy of spoliation of Jews in Nazi occupied Europe. The ALIU final report is made up of one hundred and seventy five pages and contains two types of report. Detailed Interrogation Reports (DIRs) which focus on individuals who played a pivotal role in this Nazi spoliation activity. A DIR details the network and relations between art dealers and those employed by Adolf Hitler, Herman Goering and Alfred Rosenberg the head of the ERR, with the following main protagonists all now red flagged:

Ernst Buchner – Nazi Art Administrator

Theodore Fischer – Swiss Art Dealer

Hilderbrand Gurlitt – Art Historian and Gallery Director

Karl Haberstock – Berlin Art Dealer

Walter Hofer – Director of the Goering Collection

Heinrich Hoffman – Official Photographer for Hitler

Bruno Lohse – Art dealer and SS member

Gustav Rochlitz – Art dealer for the ERR

Herman Voss – Deputy Director (designate) Fuhrer Museum

The ALIU has also published a list of red flag names in addition to those above, organising them by country: Germany, France, Switzerland, the Netherlands, Belgium, Italy, Spain, Portugal, Sweden and Luxembourg are all included. Each individuals name is followed by a description of the persons activities, their relationship with other people within the network and in many cases information concerning their arrest and/or imprisonment by Allied Forces.

Consolidated Interrogation Reports (CIRs) provide generic information on the art looting activities of Goering (for the Goering Collection) the art looting activities of Rosenberg's ERR and Hitler's Fuhrer Museum. One DIR and two CIRs, containing key intelligence, are presented at the end of this file.

Background

Adolf Hitler was an unsuccessful artist who was denied admission to the Vienna Academy of Fine Arts. In 1907 and 1908, a young Hitler who had travelled from Linz in Austria, was twice denied admission to this institution. He then stayed in Vienna, subsisting on his orphan allowance and tried unsuccessfully to continue his profession as an artist. Soon he had withdrawn into poverty and started selling amateur paintings for small amounts until he left Vienna in May 1913. He continued in his life, militarily then politically, to consider himself a connoisseur of the arts. In his book Mein Kampf (My Fight) an autobiographical Nazi party manifesto written whilst in Landsberg Prison southwest of Munich in 1925, after the failed Munich Putsch, the book describes the process by which Hitler became antisemitic and outlines his political ideology and future plans for Germany.

The Nazi regime in Germany actively promoted and censored forms of art between 1933 and 1945. Upon becoming dictator in 1933, Adolf Hitler gave his personal artistic preference the full force of law to a degree rarely seen before. In the case of Germany the model was to be classical Greek and Roman art. Seen by Hitler as an art whose exterior form embodied an inner racial ideal, that was easily comprehensible to the average German citizen, both heroic and romantic. This Nazi view of art stemmed partly from conservative aesthetics and partly from their determination to use culture as propaganda. He also ferociously attacked modern art as degenerate including Cubism, Futurism and Dadaism. All of which he personally considered the product of a decadent twentieth century society.

Cubism – where in art objects are analysed, broken up and reassembled in an abstract form

Futurism – it emphasises speed, technology, youth, violence and objects such as the car and plane

Dadaism – expressed nonsense, irrationality and anti-capitalist protest in its art

In 1933 when Hitler became Chancellor of Germany, he began enforcing these artistic ideals on the nation. In relation to paintings, the types that were favoured amongst the hierarchy of the Nazi party were classical portraits and landscapes by the Old Masters, as they are referred to. Particularly those of German origin and can be defined as a pre-eminent western European painter of the 13th - 18th centuries. Modern art that did not match this criteria was described as degenerate art by the Nazi regime and virtually everything that was found in Germany's museums was sold or destroyed. With the sums raised one of Hitler's objectives was to establish the Fuhrer Museum in Linz, Austria. Other Nazi leaders such as Luftwaffe Chief Hermann Goering and Foreign Minister Joachim von Ribbentrop were also intent on taking advantage of German military imperial success, with plans to increase their own private art collections.

Sale of Art confiscated from German Museums

German art dealers lead by the red flagged Hildebrand Gurlitt, set up a gallery just outside of Berlin to sell a cache of nearly 16000 paintings and sculptures which Hitler and Goering had authorised to be removed from the walls of German museums in 1937-38. They were first put on display in the Haus der Kunst (House of Art) a non-collecting modern art museum located in Munich on 19th July 1937. The Nazi leaders invited public mockery of the art by two million gallery visitors, who came to view the condemned modern art in the so called Degenerate Art Exhibition.

The exhibition was organised and administered by Adolf Ziegler a German painter and politician. He was tasked by the Nazi leadership to oversee the purging of all degenerate art by all German artists. He was also Hitler's favourite painter. Nazi propagandist Joseph Goebbels has in a radio broadcast called Germany's degenerate artists garbage. Hitler opened the exhibition with a speech, in it he described German art as suffering 'a great and fatal illness.' However, Hitler later ordered that all confiscated works of art were to be made directly available to him.

Public burning of Art

Hildebrand Gurlitt and his gallery associates did not have much success with their sales. Mainly because art labelled as rubbish had small appeal to any private buyer. So on 20th March 1939 they set fire to 1004 paintings and sculptures and 3825 watercolours, drawings and prints in the courtyard of the Berlin Fire Department. It was an act of infamy similar to the Nazi book burning campaign conducted in Germany and Austria in 1933, where books were ceremonially burnt that were viewed as subversive or representing views opposed to Nazism. This particular propaganda act raised the financial attention for which they had hoped. The Basel Museum in Switzerland arrived soon after with 50,000 francs to spend. Shocked art lovers came to buy. What our intelligence shows is that after these sales it is unknown how many of the panting/drawings/sculptures have been kept by Gurlitt and his associates. But they have indeed sold to buyers in Switzerland and America for their own financial gain.

Public Auctions and Private Sales in Switzerland

The most notorious auction of Nazi looted art was a degenerate art auction organised by the red flagged Theodore Fischer on 30th June 1939, at the National Grand Hotel in Lucerne, Switzerland. The artwork on offer had been officially deaccessioned from German museums by the Nazi regime, yet many well-known private art dealers participated alongside agents for major collectors and buyers from foreign museums. However, intelligence indicated that many of the sales had in fact taken place in private and the public auctions can now be considered a public relations exercise for the German people and a smoke screen by the regime. Research and careful documentation has already begun by the Office of Strategic Services regarding the role of Switzerland as an art dealing centre and conduit for cultural assets, during the Nazi regime and in the immediate post-war period.

ERR, Fuhrer Museum and Hermann Goering

Whilst the regime systematically stole cultural property from Germany itself and from every territory they occupied, this was undertaken by two key institutions and primarily one Nazi leader. They were both the drivers and decision makers specifically who determined which private and public collections were deemed as the most valuable and culturally desirable to the Nazi propaganda. The Einstazstab Reichsleiter Rosenberg (ERR) or in English the Reich Rosenberg Taskforce was formed in 1940 and headed by Alfred Rosenberg. However, intelligence indicates the ERR was in reality controlled by Herman Goering. This organisation had the sole remit of identifying and then acquiring by any means necessary cultural property in whatever form.

Adolf Hitler began making plans to transform his home city of Linz, in Austria, almost immediately after he became Chancellor and prior to him taking full control of Germany. It was to become the Third Reich capital city for the arts. Hitler appointed architects and ordered them to work from some of his own designs, to build several galleries and museums which would collectively be known as the Fuhrer Museum. He wanted to fill the museum with the greatest art treasures in the world and believed that most of the finest art in the world belonged to Germany, after having been stolen during the Napoleonic Wars and World War I.

The Hermann Goering collection, a personal collection of the Chief-of-Staff, was a very large collection. It has been identified by the ALIU as containing around fifty percent of art confiscated from the enemies of the Nazi regime. Assembled in large part by the red flagged art dealer Bruno Loshe, Goering's advisor and ERR representative in Paris. As of 1945 the collection included over 2,000 individual pieces of which there were more than 300 paintings.

ERR vs MFAA

Rosenberg and the ERR task force were operationally extremely busy stealing works of art from Jewish families, art museums and other collections all over Europe. From 1943 the MFAA was on the ground working hard to recover art and antiquities assisted by Allied Forces. They were a specialist group of three hundred and forty five people mostly from the art and museum world. After the surrender of Germany they were able to methodically search out works of art that the Nazis had hidden.

At times the MFAA mission was very fortunate. During a visit to a dentist in a city in the west of Germany by two unit members for one to have treatment, the dentist heard about their remit and so introduced them to his son-in-law. The young German had helped the Nazis to steal works of art and was now eager to get his family out of Germany to Paris. As a bargaining tool he told the two members of MFAA about a large storage facility in the Altausee Salt Mine. Two months later the MFAA were the first to crawl through the dark tunnels of this strategically important mine.

Crucially, this mine was not far from the Eagles Nest, the alpine resort of Hitler. It was the main storage facility for the art that Hitler had selected for his upcoming Fuhrer Museum. Altausee had partly been fitted out with a storage room comprising wooden floors and modern lighting which is essential when dealing with paintings and dehumidifiers. No less than 6577 paintings, 2300 drawings or watercolours, 137 sculptures, 954 art prints and 12-1700 boxes of books were stored in the mine.

MFAA Recovery Operations and Nazi Storage Locations

Stolen art and antiquities were stored in deep mines and in castles throughout Germany and Austria, where the treasures would primarily be safe from allied bombing. They were ideal storage locations as many were up to depths of eight hundred metres and most were part of a sprawling network of tunnels capable of providing huge storage capacity. Their interiors provided stable atmospheric moisture and temperature conditions, commensurate with the long term storage of art and antiquities. Many of the hidden works were both of high value and culturally important, but not all the art and antiquities stolen have been located at this time.

April 1945

In a salt mine in Thuringia Germany the MFAA salvaged gold bars worth $200 million, sacks of foreign currency and works of art including the bust of the Egyptian Queen Nefertiti.

April 1945

While the war still raged through the streets of Nuremberg they salvaged some of the local museums antiquities. Among the valuables recovered was a national treasure belonging to Poland. The thirteen metre high oak and larch wood fifteenth century Veit Stoss altarpiece stolen in 1941 from Krakow.

May 1945

In a salt mine in Ransbach, Thuringia, Germany the MFAA found over two million books, manuscripts and maps from the former Prussian state library in Berlin. The mine also stored notebooks and costumes from the Berlin State Opera and a large quantity of paintings from the state museum in Berlin.

May 1945

In a salt mine in Bernterode, Thuringia, Germany the MFAA found crown jewels belonging to the German House of Hohenzollern, the imperial royal dynasty.

May 1945

The MFAA discovered the aforementioned famous artwork in the Altausee mine, Austria.

May 1945

In the underground tunnels above which was the Eagles Nest, from where Hitler directed most of the war, the MFAA found more than one thousand paintings and sculptures. They had been collected by Hermann Goering and included works by the famous seventeenth century painters Rubens, Titian and van Dyck.

ART CRIME AND SECURITY

May 1945

Enough art, antiquities and gold to fill six US Army trucks was uncovered by the MFAA in a church in northern Italian town of San Leonardo.

May 1945

In the Siegen copper mine Germany, the MFFA found the Charlemagne antiquities from Aachen Cathedral Germany one of the oldest roman catholic churches in Europe. They also uncovered paintings, sculptures, manuscripts and antiquities stolen from other German museums.

May 1945

The MFAA discovered about six thousand works of art, jewellery and furniture at Neuschwanstein Castle, Germany, most of these had been stolen from French collectors.

May 1945

In the monastery in Buxheim, Bavaria, the MFAA discovered nineteenth century antiquities and furniture from Russia and Oriental rugs and textiles. There were also one hundred and fifty eight paintings including those by Goya, Delacroix and Renoir. It was also found to be a main operational base for ERR operations with conservation and restoration rooms for its stolen antiquities. A cleverly hidden but strategically important base for the repair of art works.

Art and Antiquities Still Missing

The Amber Room

Was installed in the Catherine Palace in St Petersburg during the 1700s. Its panels included 450kg of amber, gold and jewels valued at more than £380 million today. When the Germans invaded the Soviet Union they plundered the chamber and sent the valuables back to Germany, location still unknown.

Paintings

The Nazis moved a large collection of paintings, including works by van Gough to a salt mine 30km outside Magdeburg. During an Allied bombing on the city in 1945 it is thought this resulted in a fire breaking out in the mine and those works are now believed destroyed.

The King of Poland Treasure

A casket of jewellery belonging to the Polish royal family disappeared in 1939 in Nazi occupied south-eastern Poland. It was then stored with other collections from the Czartoryski Museum and there is no current intelligence as to where those jewels might be.

Gold Bullion

This bullion has vanished from Germany. The Nazis stole this gold from wealthy families and sent it abroad to buy war material. Much of the gold has not been found. Whether it is hidden in mines, lakes, castle vaults or has been laundered is unknown. No reliable intelligence is currently available.

Current ALIU Interrogation Reports

As part of the remit of the ALIU and to explain discoveries already made the MFAA in the field, a series of interrogations on individuals believed to be involved in art and antiquities looting were completed. These then complimented a set of reports outlining the biographies and activities of these persons and the Nazi elite. They had then distributed them to the various Allied government agencies, and the temporary governments of those countries invaded.

The two Nazi leaders most related to the practice and who become as the war progressed, somewhat adversarial, were Adolf Hitler and his appointed successor Hermann Goering. The latter it could be argued was the main protagonist. Hitler committed suicide in his bunker after the fall of Berlin and his body burnt. Goering was taken prisoner by the US Seventh Army in Bavaria. It is believed Goering had made his way to US lines in the hope of surrendering into the custody of the Allies, rather than to the Soviets, no doubt fearing what they would have done to him. The ALIU reports build a broad picture of their art collections and intentions as well as the acquisition methods they used. The following three interrogation reports have been selected for this file as they provide a succinct overview of how those involved thought and acted in relation to Hitler, the Fuhrer Museum, the Goering collection and the art dealers that helped and advised them.

Consolidated Interrogation Report No.4 – Fuhrer Museum

This report lays out the context which underpinned the majority of the art Hitler collected, that being the Fuhrer Museum and Library. Linz in Austria has featured heavily in his post war plans as the cultural centre of Europe and to act as his legacy. An array of public buildings, including a mausoleum to house his tomb, were designed directly from his own plans and at the centre of his modern industrial metropolis was to stand an art gallery like no other - the Fuhrer Museum. The type of artwork Hitler pursued stood to legitimise the Nazi regime. His collection was a focus on German and Austrian art and seventy five percent of that collection was made up of Old Masters, with images of muscular and racially pure figures.

To realise his ambition the Linz project had its own special budget and department - Special Commission: Linz. This was initially funded by profits from his book and the royalties from his image on postage stamps. Looting played a major role in his strategy and as a result of his extensive buying and looting, art market prices were heavily inflated during the war years. Ironically, at a time that saw very strict commodity prices and supply issues across the world. His obsession continued to the end, with one of the last pictures of him in the Berlin bunker admiring his replica of a Linz City.

Consolidated Interrogation Report No.2 – Hermann Goering

This report focuses on the collecting activities of Hermann Goering, as members of the ERR begun to work solely in the interests of Goering above Hitler. He was interested in building up an art collection for himself and thus began contradicting the orders of Hitler, using ERR activities for his own interests. He ensured that he was the first to examine stolen art and make the decisions on what was to be done with the pieces. Whilst all art looted by the ERR was ordered to be sent directly to Hitler, only about fifty three works made it into the Linz Museum collection in waiting. Goering on the other hand has amassed over seven hundred objects via ERR activities. As the head of the Luftwaffe he could supply the ERR with transport and military personnel that they were not able to source elsewhere.

Most striking is the fact that Goering has spent an extraordinary amount of time looking for works of art, even in the most crucial years of the war. He made trips displacing his entire staff and the Nazi elite Special Train, solely for the purpose of visiting art dealers who had art he wanted. The image of having an extensive and impressive art collection was an effort to project himself as an aristocratic man of culture. Upon his capture at

Nuremberg he freely and proudly boasted that he owned the finest art collection in all of Europe.

Detailed Interrogation Report No.12 – Hermann Voss

This report focuses on Hermann Voss the Deputy Director (designate) of the Fuhrer Museum project and red flagged by the ALIU. To properly facilitate the Nazi elite to amass works of art on this scale it required extensive planning, expertise and logistical resources. This meant enlisting the help of art historians, dealers and commercial galleries. In fact hundreds of experts from the art world have been employed in helping carry out these operations. He was previously the director of a small museum in Wiesbaden southwest of Frankfurt. During the interrogation he made sure to present himself as staunch anti-Nazi. However, his subsequent appointment was believed unusual by the ALIU for a man running such a small museum with an anti-Nazi viewpoint, to suddenly be given such an exalted position. Considering what Hitler's art collecting priorities were, access to the best of the best was the deciding factor in such matters. What is unexpected was the ability of the Nazi elite to so easily engage with those opposed to their political ideology, with so many claiming fear in any refusal to cooperate

To seemingly offer explanation to the ALIU on this account, Voss claimed he took the post with the view of protecting cultural property and that he was unaware of the management and scope of the Linz project. Including its involvement with confiscated works before he became Deputy Director. On learning the Linz collection did indeed contain confiscated works, Voss declared that he had determined to do what he could to keep other looted works from being added to the collection.

However, works in which Voss had complete knowledge were two hundred and fifty pictures from the French-Jewish Schloss collection, of which he was alerted to the circumstances in discussions prior to receipt of the works. During the interrogation on this Voss' memory conveniently fails him on the details. Voss was in the end of the view that confiscated paintings were sure to go somewhere, so what difference did it make. Voss' story is a similar one to the many art specialists involved in Nazi art collecting. Red flagged Ernest Buchner was one of countless prominent German men, who in spite of their inner dislike of Nazism and a realisation of its evils, nevertheless agreed to act as one of its representatives. Through a mixture of personal ambition and fear of the consequences of standing aside, they both helped to fulfil the desires of the Nazi elite and aided their strategy. The report concludes that Voss, Buchner and others are men that bear a heavy responsibility to the mass of their compatriots. For they provided the fanatics and criminals that were the Nazi elite, with that necessary cloak of responsibility.

Chapter 2
Art and Law

Art law can be defined as a body of law which would include domestic and foreign law, along with multilateral treaties, conventions and regulations that are applied to fine art and cultural property. It can be argued that art in law is not given its full attention by the criminal justice system. This is a complicated legal definition because of the international dimension of the art market and dealers. Criminal law varies country to country and within territories and is further complicated by their own unique makeup, structure and workings. Generally, specialist art lawyers will negotiate, litigate and advise clients on the full range of legal issues that arise concerning works of art and the art markets. These would include, art dealer and auctioneer duties and rights, authenticity disputes, works of art and their provenance, loans of artwork to museums and exhibition agreements, stolen works of art, looted and confiscated works of art from the Nazi era.

A mix of legal elements in any art proceedings or enquiries can prove difficult and protracted but is particular prevalent around the issue of authenticity and the introduction of fake art and antiquities into the marketplace. However, we also know the market loves a discovery, a deal, that will always be too good for one buyer to resist. With art experts examining large quantities of art it has been suggested as much as forty percent could be misattributed. The counter argument being that when you deal with extremely old art and antiquity most of it has probably been attributed as best it could be with the historical, provenance, scientific and art expert analysis available at the time. There are two major forms that a deception can take. One is for the faker to duplicate an existing work or the other to create an imagined reproduction thereby duplicating the style of a particular artist. However, this is not done to recreate a specific work but rather to create that undiscovered masterpiece, coming to light amid a media frenzy, just as we have seen with the work of Han van Meegeren.

So the issue of authenticity versus fraud in the guise of fake art and forged provenance documents, underscores the difference between the art market with their concern for authenticity and the criminal justice system with its legal concern for fraud and the requisite evidential elements needing to be present for any law enforcement investigation or criminal prosecution to proceed, let alone be successful. What will be the bedrock of any prosecution is whether a given piece of art or antiquity can be demonstrated to be a fake. With the narrative previously described in the fake, forgeries and science chapter it is here the courts must turn to art experts and scientific examiners for assistance. However, this needs to be coupled with other criteria to complete the legal requirements.

Within the legal world the concepts of an identified victim who has suffered a financial loss or injury is the starting point for any law enforcement activity. But especially in the world of art as the act of a deception with the requisite mental knowledge can be more difficult to prove. It is the actus reus, the action or conduct which is the physical act of committing a crime (by selling the art) coupled with the mens rea, the mental knowledge or intention of committing a crime (by deceiving the buyer as to its authenticity) and both elements must be present for a crime to be complete. As you can imagine this would be a high threshold for other crime such as theft or assault but even more so in relation to proving the sale of fake art and antiquities. There can be a number of quite unique circumstances when this threshold is not met if we work on the basis that the word fake conveys both the physical element of a piece of art or antiquity and the presence of the mental element of the crime. However, there are three opposing areas of mitigation for this, the opinion of art experts, the original artist and their methods of working and conservation techniques.

There are times when the term fake can be applied despite there being no provable intention to deceive a buyer. After the examination by art experts and scientific examiners art can be upgraded as well as downgraded and quite literally, has been. So something purchased with a disputed provenance may be upgraded, likewise something bought as the real deal may be subsequently downgraded and this would apply to museums, commercial galleries and private collectors. There are numerous circumstances when a work can be without doubt a fake but there is no hint of dishonesty by the suspect. This can be seen when a buyer who bought fake art in good faith and as completely authentic, then sells it on as such, the necessary mental legal element would clearly not be present and therefore the necessary legal twin elements of a crime incomplete.

The famous artist in question may have painted many different versions of the same scene or occasionally spurious additions had been made by them, that might cloud the authenticity issue at the heart of any investigation or prosecution. There are also instances in which unfinished or abandoned works of one artist have been finished by another. The famous artist may have painted a masterpiece at the time but which was then copied by one or more of their apprentice assistants. For example, The Last Supper by Leonardo da Vinci covers an end wall of the dining hall at the monastery of Santa Maria delle Grazie in Milan, Italy. Two early copies of The Last Supper are known to exist and are indeed only presumed to be the work of assistants. The copies are almost the size of the original and have survived with a wealth of original detail still intact. One, by Giampietrino is in the collection of the Royal Academy of Arts, London and the other by Cesare da Sesto at the Church of St. Ambrogio in Ponte Capriasca, Switzerland. A third copy is painted by Andrea Solari and is on display in the Leonardo da Vinci Museum at Tongerlo Abbey in Belgium. The point here being that you have three paintings completed in the 1500s, two by his assistants, that provide you with versions of a painting that will stand up to scientific examination and in the case of his assistant painters who studied his technique and tried hard to replicate it exactly. This then means that additional versions of a painting could indeed be completed by the original artist and thus a situation where experts are unable to agree on the definitive status of the work in question.

Conservation in art and antiquities can inadvertently introduce the problem of alterations in fake art prosecutions. Probably the most common form of alteration occurs in the legitimate and sometimes much needed process of restoration and conservation. Some of the restorations are so extensive that there will inevitably be questions about how much of the work was done by the original artist. The borderline between extensive restoration and fake art is difficult to draw and some restoration has even taken place by previous civilisations in relation to antiquities. The problem for the art experts, scientific examiners and the court is to determine if the restoration work has been so extensive that the work may no longer be viewed, properly, as authentic.

Chapter 3
Repatriation and Recovery

In the art world the term repatriation mean the process of giving back cultural objects, generally antiquities, that were taken from indigenous groups during times of occupation, colonialism and other dark periods of imperialism. As well as looted antiquities, which have been smuggled out of the source country and then traded on the main international art markets. The term recovery refers to the restitution of, generally art, to their legal owner or heir. That is the owner recovers what they once owned, what was taken from them. As we know there are many problems besetting legal efforts to secure the return of stolen art and antiquities. After a theft or looting the object can cross numerous borders and travel through many legal jurisdictions, most of which have different legal structures governing the fate of the stolen art, whatever its final destination may be. We also know there are significant legal hurdles facing foreign institutions or governments for the repatriation of antiquities and those individuals claiming for the return of stolen art. The sometimes lengthy and as we shall see, important passage of time since the original theft, looting or the now challenged legitimacy of a sale. Then the unwillingness on the part of the eventual owner of the art or antiquity to return it voluntarily. There has also long been a reluctance on the part of legal systems worldwide to accord enforcement of the rules or judgements of another foreign legal system, resulting in largely uneven and inadequate dispute resolution.

Repatriation

When you consider source countries for lost antiquities such as Egypt, Greece and Peru it was during times of conquest and empire building that indigenous civilisations were deprived of their land and freedom. At the same time, the invaders help themselves to the cultural riches of the said territories. The purchasing and collecting of those in the early 19th and 20th centuries by travelling abroad, be it on behalf of museums or wealthy private collectors were completed under extremely suspect arrangements. Sometimes the real loss of tangible heritage means each sacred indigenous antiquity in a foreign museum represents hundreds of stories and memories lost. Many indigenous people are left feeling that the continued, centuries spanning, presence in western museums of antiquity acquired by whatever means, seems to validate the various ways in which they were taken. However, repatriating cultural antiquities will not change the past, as it can be argued the damage has already been done. But still better the reimagining and display of antiquities in their rightful place of their source country, than keeping the antiquity in a box in a museum far away.

Recovery

During times of extreme political and social upheaval museums, institutions, churches and private collectors have been forced to part with their art. Recovery of art is at its most prominent when referencing the return of art and antiquities taken from the Jewish people of Germany and other Nazi occupied countries during World War II. The so-called Holocaust art cases are an important part of contemporary debate and legal activities concerning recovery. It is therefore important to understand both the scale of the crimes and the implications that the recovery of Holocaust art has had on the art market. Before and during their attempt to eradicate all Jewish people the Nazis eagerly sought to acquire their assets and among these assets were art.

As part of the Allied Armies post war administration of Nazi occupied countries in Europe, relating to art recovered by the Allies, it was agreed stolen art and antiquities would be returned to their country of origin in the first instance. The Allied Armies already appointed interim governments of those nations would then separately administer and facilitate the return of all relevant art to either their national museums, non-national museums, galleries or private collectors. This was because the Allied Armies had more pressing military and security matters to resolve, but it can be argued that this arrangement, for whatever reasons, did not work and as a result much art was never rightfully or correctly returned. Owners who had been forced to flee to other countries or murdered but no enquiries were made to track down possible heirs. Thus, thousands and thousands of art and antiquities entered national collections or the art market with a stain on their provenance and a suspicious ownership gap. Subsequent buyers of such art faced enduring possibilities that the true owner or heir would, sooner or later, come forward and that a court would rule for the restitution of that art. As a result there are many cases of dubious art dealers and buyers creating false provenance documents to cover Holocaust-era gaps. All this despite the heroic wartime efforts of the Allied Armies and units such as the Monuments Men.

The issues of state crime becomes important when you have art plunder of the likes of that during the war years. In criminology the concept of state crime recognises that it is not just individuals or corporations who can act criminally but political regimes in charge of states. State crime can be defined as actions that break the states own criminal law or public international law. For a regime to commit those crimes action usually covers the areas of crimes by national security forces e.g. genocide, torture, imprisonment without trial and disappearance of dissidents. Political Crimes e.g. censorship or corruption, economic crimes e.g. violation of health and safety laws and social and cultural crimes e.g. institutional racism all crimes without doubt committed by the Nazi regime. Contemporary recognition of state crimes tends to involve looking at state violations mirrored by way of internationally accepted norms of conduct, particularly human rights standards.

We can see examples of this form of state crime in the forced sales of art during World War II. The Nazis and others who participated in the looting did so under laws brought in once they took power. Other art was taken into national ownership, again under specific new legislation. In other cases, the owners were forced to part with art to pay for massive completely invented taxes that were only applied to the Jewish population of whatever country. The art was always, unsurprisingly, undervalued by the Nazis and in one way or another people were forced to sign away their ownership. The Nazis were then meticulous in their documentation of the newly acquired art, as much of the art taken was meant for internal resale within Germany or external sale, with the hope of generating much needed foreign currency. The Nazis were acutely aware that stolen art without any paperwork, without proof of provenance or legal transfer of ownership had little value. The fact that such a paper trail existed was both a blessing and a curse for provenance researchers and the families of victims who are seeking the recovery of the art. Disagreement over interpretation of records related to art seizure and sales are at the very core of many recovery proceedings. Two classic examples of this are the theft by the Nazis of the Gustav Klimt painting the Woman in Gold (as previously described in chapter one) and the Max Leibermann work Two Riders on the Beach.

Max Leibermann was born in 1847 in Berlin Germany, to wealthy Jewish parents and he became particularly famous for his portraits of which more than two hundred were commissioned over his lifetime. Two Riders on the Beach is the title of two similar paintings that Liebermann painted in 1901 and both of these paintings are considered masterpieces of German art. One of the versions was subsequently bought by David Friedmann a wealthy Jewish industrialist. The art collection of Friedmann was seized and subject to a Nazis inventory in 1939 and assigned a value of 10,785 Reichsmarks (though it was estimated to be worth ten to fifteen times that) with Two Riders on the Beach alone estimated to be able to reach 10,000 to 15,000 Reichsmarks if sold abroad.

Two Riders on the Beach was eventually acquired along with most of the Friedmann collection by the German art dealer and collector Hildebrand Gurlitt. No complete pre-Nazi inventory of the Friedmann collection is known to exist and if it did, was no doubt destroyed during the Nazi regime. As we know Gurlitt was highlighted in the OSS 1945 file, was a red flagged individual of high interest and he kept this particular painting until the end of the war. Though the Allied Armies Monuments Men had seized the work along with other art held by Gurlitt after World War II, they returned the collection when Gurlitt no doubt using his art expertise and knowledge, convinced them he was the rightful owner. In 2012 German police executed a warrant to search the Munich apartment of Cornelius Gurlitt after a couple of years investigation into his art dealings. Cornelius was the son of Hildebrand Gurlitt and had been entrusted by his father with the care of his collection of 121 framed and 1,285 unframed artworks. When the police entered his reasonably small apartment they found works by Picasso, Matisse, Renoir and many others. They also found both of the long lost Two Riders on the Beach paintings owned by Friedmann.

Development of international law relating to art recovery begins with the two tribunals established in Nuremberg by the

Allies between 1945 and 1949. The first and better known tribunal, effectively a court, indicted twenty four major Nazi leaders which resulted in nineteen convictions, of which twelve led to death sentences and three acquittals. There were then no new developments in this arena for another fifty years until 1998 when the important Washington Conference Principles on Nazi-confiscated art were released. It was agreement on protocols of how countries, museums, galleries, private collectors and the heirs of those affected, should deal with the immense legal and social problem of Nazi looted art available on the art market. They consist of a list of eleven principles that are meant to represent the best practise for one hundred and ninety-three countries dealing with those art recovery cases. Many countries including Germany, signed up to these principles committing to them within the context of their own laws, the principles are as follows.

Art that had been confiscated by the Nazis and not subsequently restituted should be identified.

Relevant records and archives should be open and accessible to researchers in accordance with the guidelines of the International Council on Archives.

Resources and personnel should be made available to facilitate the identification of all art that had been confiscated by the Nazis and not subsequently restituted.

In establishing that a work of art had been confiscated by the Nazis and not subsequently restituted, consideration should be given to unavoidable gaps or ambiguities in the provenance in light of the passage of time and the circumstances of the Holocaust era.

Every effort should be made to publicise art that is found to have been confiscated by the Nazis and not subsequently restituted in order to locate its pre-war owners or their heirs.

Efforts should be made to establish a central registry of such information.

Pre-war owners and their heirs should be encouraged to come forward and make known their claims to art that was confiscated by the Nazis and not subsequently restituted.

If the pre-war owners of art that is found to have been confiscated by the Nazis and not subsequently restituted or their heirs can be identified, steps should be taken expeditiously to achieve a just and fair solution recognizing this may vary according to the facts and circumstances surrounding a specific case.

If the pre-war owners of art that is found to have been confiscated by the Nazis or their heirs, cannot be identified steps should be taken expeditiously to achieve a just and fair solution.

Commissions or other bodies established to identify art that was confiscated by the Nazis and to assist in addressing ownership issues should have a balanced membership.

Nations are encouraged to develop national processes to implement these principles, particularly as they relate to other dispute resolution mechanisms for resolving ownership issues.

Despite the conference principles and increased international cooperation, there is still a continued absence of real effective international law when stolen art is situated overseas at the time of any claim and in those countries where legal systems seem to be more sympathetic for the current owners to retain the art. This approach seems to be in a greater abundance when the art is currently under the control of, for example, a countries national museum and when that piece of art or antiquity is popular with the national population. This we have seen in the Woman in Gold case, where the painting was deemed to be an Austrian national treasure and the authorities fought hard to keep it as such.

When the recovery of stolen art and antiquity is sought in the legal sphere the obstacle of time limitation periods frequently arises as a prime obstacle. When stolen art has been out of circulation for many years and is located the law requires a demand and refusal approach, so as long as the owner has had continuous possession of the art for a least three years they can refuse to return it. Once a lawful approach and demand has been received and then unequivocally refused a legal time limitation period is imposed and must expire before any claim will be statue barred. This will vary internationally and by legal jurisdiction. For example in the UK, certain US states and all but one state in Australia it is six years and in some countries this time period would renew each time the painting is sold. So to recap, an heir wishes to claim recovery of a painting and the current owner has over three year ownership, the claimant now has six years in which to bring proceedings and contest ownership of the art.

The same position in terms of limitation would still apply in respect of looted antiquities with no known owner but with evidence as to its cultural origin, with the originating country equal to an individual private claimant. Such cases are usually brought before the courts of the country where the item is currently located, with issues of ownership rightly determined by the application of the laws of the country where the item was originally discovered, looted and then illegally exported. Legal proceedings would then require calling expert evidence as to the laws of the state of origin by lawyers acting on behalf of the government making the claim. UK and US courts, for example, have shown a willingness to give effective credence to a nations national heritage laws and desire for repatriation of antiquities and the individuals recovery of stolen art. However, it is still a universal problem without a universal solution. As stolen art is traced and so to the affected governments demand for the repatriation, disputes will continue to come before the courts. It will continue to require a simplicity of approach and a fair and consistent application of legal principles across international borders.

Methods and Sources

As I alluded to in the preface of this book, the ideas and compilation presented here are introductory. I have sought to spark initial interest in the reader by giving an overview of five famous thefts, which are then better put into context by subsequent chapters. As an author I also seek to keep to the subject matter and move that subject matter along, in a chronological fashion. There are too many books that spend too much time meandering along, over a number of excessive pages but with no payback for that extra page turning. I have sought out different sources for this book but not so many sources that the information is repeating itself, thereby not providing the reader with any further benefit. I gratefully acknowledge the following for their organisational archival material or individuals for their specific, expert and enlightening views on the subject matter. These sources are listed alphabetically.

Maria Altman, Walter Alva, Martin Bale, Duncan Chappell, Noah Charney, Jorun Christoffersen, Jerome Coignard, Catherine Deely, Morten Ervik, Tom Johansen, Michel van Rijn, Simon Mackenzie, Kenneth Polk, Giovanni Pastore, Charles Sabba, Donald Sassoon, Randol Schoenberg, Thomas Seydou, Margeaux Sippell, Angelo Tartuferi, Arthur Thompkins, Don Thompson, International Foundation for Art Research, UK Council for Museums, Archives and Libraries and last but by no means least, the excellent United States National Archives.

www.ingramcontent.com/pod-product-compliance
Lightning Source LLC
Chambersburg PA
CBHW020654220526
45464CB00001B/426